Anonymous

Historical Sketches of the County of Elgin

Anonymous

Historical Sketches of the County of Elgin

ISBN/EAN: 9783337013264

Printed in Europe, USA, Canada, Australia, Japan

Cover: Foto ©ninafisch / pixelio.de

More available books at **www.hansebooks.com**

HISTORICAL SKETCHES

OF THE

COUNTY OF ELGIN

PUBLISHED BY

THE ELGIN HISTORICAL AND SCIENTIFIC INSTITUTE.

ST. THOMAS, ONT.
THE TIMES PRINT.
1895.

PREFACE.

The Elgin Historical and Scientific Institute was established on the 29th day of April, 1891. One of its principal objects is that of collecting and preserving records and memorials of the early history of the County of Elgin. The public have shown a sympathetic interest in the work. By voluntary contributions the nucleus of a library and museum has been formed which it is hoped will in time grow to considerable dimensions.

The Institute, in now issuing its first volume, desires to recognize the generous and public spirited action of the Council of the County of Elgin in voting a sum to defray the expenses of publication.

Persons having old letters, books or manuscripts relating to the early settlement of the County, or any archæological remains of the aboriginal inhabitants, are requested to deposit them with the Institute. If the owners would prefer not to part with the property in such articles, the Institute would be glad to take charge of them as custodian for the owners for such period as the latter may desire.

The special thanks of the Institute are due to the Very Reverend Dean Harris, author of The History of the Early Missions in Western Canada, to the Librarian of the Legislative Assembly for Ontario, and Messrs. D. McColl, ex-M. P. P., H. B. Donly, Richard Locker and others, for courtesies in connection with the preparation and publication of this book.

St. Thomas, June 1st, 1895.

OFFICERS
Elgin Historical and Scientific Institute
1891.

James H. Coyne	President
Judge Ermatinger	Vice-President
W. H. Murch	Secretary
J. S. Robertson	Treasurer
F. Hunt	Editor
K. W. McKay	Librarian
Frank L. Farley	Curator

COUNCIL
J. Wilkinson, W. R. Jackson, J. S. Brierley,
A. W. Campbell, and W. Atkin.

1892

Judge Ermatinger	President
Dr. H. H. Way	Vice-President
W. H. Murch	Secretary
K. W. McKay	Treasurer
J. H. Coyne	Editor
J. W. Stewart	Curator and Librarian

COUNCIL
W. Atkin, J. S. Robertson, W. R. Jackson, A. W. Campbell
J. S. Brierley, J. Wilkinson, F. Hunt.

1893-4.

K. W. McKay	President
W. Atkin	Vice President
W. H. Murch	Secretary
J. A. Bell	Treasurer
J. W. Stewart	Librarian and Curator
Judge Ermatinger	Editor

COUNCIL
J. H. Coyne, J. S. Robertson, W. R. Jackson, A. W. Campbell, J. S. Brierley, J. Wilkinson, F. Hunt, Dr. Way.

ELGIN HISTORICAL AND SCIENTIFIC INSTITUTE.

LIST OF MEMBERS.

Atkin, W.
Brierley, J. S.
Bell, James A.
Coyne, Jas. H.
Campbell, A. W.
Doyle, Matthew
Ermatinger, Judge
Ford, N. W.
Gilbert, M. A.
Glasgow, Chas.
Hunt, Frank
Hughes, Judge
Henderson, Chester
Jackson, W. R.
Jell, H. F.
Kains, John A.
Murch, W. H.

Moore N. W.
Marshall, John
McAdam, Jos.
McKay, K. W.
McKenzie, Geo.
McCausland, Jno.
McDougall, Colin
McLennan, J. C.
Oakes, Chas.
Robertson, J. S.
Stewart, J. W.
Stacey, Jno.
Suffel, Geo.
Sutherland, Peter
Wilkinson, J.
Way, Dr. H. H.

CONTENTS.

THE COUNTRY OF THE NEUTRALS.

The Southwold Earthwork, 1—THE NEUTRALS. De Laroche-Daillon's visit in 1626, 3—Brebeuf and Chaumonot's Visit in 1640-1, 7—Champlain's Account of the Neutrals in 1616, 9—Lalemant's Account of the Neutrals in 1641, 12—The Iroquois attack the Neutrals 1650-1, 18—THE IROQUOIS' HUNTING GROUND, 20—French Exploration, 21—Dollier De Casson and Galinee, 1669-70, 21—Stimulating effect of their exploration, 23—Kettle Creek (Tonty River), 23, 27, 28—The Indian Title, Cession by the Iroquois, 1701, 28—Cession by the Mississagas, 1784, 29—Cession by the Chippawas, etc., 1790, 29—Charlevoix' visit in 1721. Describes the North Shore, 29—THE BRITISH OCCUPATION. Land Board at Detroit, 32—Patrick McNiff's Exploration. On Lake Erie "Settlement Impossible," 32—Lieutenant-Governor Simcoe, 33—His journey to Detroit, 1793, 34—Site of London selected for his capital, 33, 34, 36, 39, 42—The Winter-express; Traders; Land-hunters, 41—McNiff's map of the Thames, 1793, 42—Detroit surrendered to the United States, 1796, 34. 38, 43, —COLONEL TALBOT, 44—Settles at Port Talbot, 1803, 44—State of Settlement at that date.

THE TALBOT SETTLEMENT.

Colonel Talbot's birth and ancestry, 1—Colonel Talbot's early career, 2—Colonel Talbot and the Duke of Wellington, 2—Colonel Talbot's arrival in Canada, 1790, 2—Secretary to Governor Simcoe, 2—Application for land grant, 1803. 2—Governor Simcoe's letter, 3—Lands comprised in first grant, 4—Aim and object, 5—Extent of settlement, 6,—Conditions of settlement, 7—Roads and road making, 7—Mode of recording allotments, 8—War of 1812-15 raids on settlement, 10, 11,—An early settler's experiences, 12—Early prices, 13—Courts and court houses, 15—Turkey Point, 15—Vittoria, 15—London, 15—Sandwich, 16—Death of Colonel Talbot, 16.

DEVELOPMENT OF THE COUNTY OF ELGIN.

Origin of Local Government, 1—Canada, 5—Quebec 1763 to 1788, 6—District of Hesse 1788 to 1792, 7—U. E. Loyalists, 8 Western District 1792 to 1798, 9—London District 1800 to 1837, 14—Organization, 14—Proceedings of courts 1800, 14—Turkey Point, 36—The London District, 36—Courts, 37—Records, 37—Court of Requests, 37—Vittoria, 37—London, 39, County of Middlesex 1837 to 1852, 41—County of Elgin, 43.

APPENDIX.

List of Surveys.
List of Parliamentary Representatives.
List of Wardens.
Municipal Nomenclature.

ILLUSTRATIONS.

Galinee's Map of 1670.
Portrait of Colonel Talbot.
Portrait of Thomas Locker.

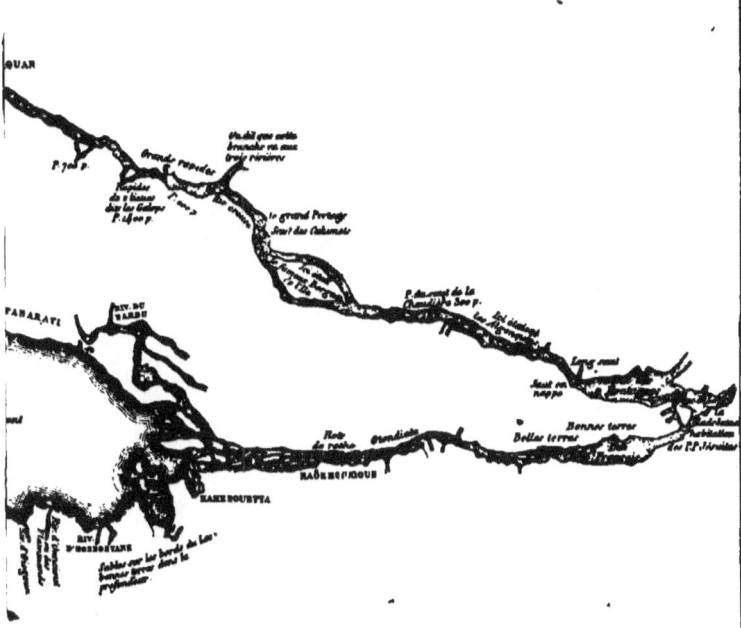

CARTE

QUE M.M. DOLLIER DE CASSON ET DE GALINEE, MISSIONNAIRES DE S.T SULPICE,

ONT PARCOURU.

Dressée par le même M.r de Galinée

(Voir La lettre de M.r Talon du 10 Novembre 1670.)

ncaise," and in "The History of the Early Missions in Western Canada." mentioned book.

gan or Fresh-water Sea of the Hurons." (These lakes were erroneously supposed to be but one), of the Iroquois, which we broke up and threw into the water." ESSEX PENINSULA : "Large prairies," ver or Tina-Toua." EAST SIDE GRAND RIVER : "Excellent land." WEST SIDE GRAND RIVER (up gara) Falls said by the Indians to be more than 200 feet high." LAKE ONTARIO : "I passed

THE COUNTRY OF THE NEUTRALS.
BY
JAMES H. COYNE.

In that part of the township of Southwold included in the peninsula between Talbot Creek and the most westerly bend of Kettle Creek there were until a comparatively recent date several Indian earthworks, which were well-known to the pioneers of the Talbot Settlement. What the tooth of time had spared for more than two centuries yielded however to the settler's plough and harrow, and but one or two of these interesting reminders of an almost forgotten race remain to gratify the curiosity of the archæologist or of the historian. Fortunately, the most important of all is still almost in its original condition. It is that, which has become known to readers of the Transactions of the Canadian Institute as the Southwold Earthwork. It is situated on the farm of Mr. Chester Henderson, Lot Number Four North on Talbot Road East. Mr. David Boyle in the Archæological Reports printed in 1891 has given the results of his examinations of the mounds. A carefully prepared plan made from actual survey by Mr. A. W. Campbell, C. E., for the Elgin Historical and Scientific Institute of St. Thomas, was presented by the latter to the Canadian Institute. (a) These will together form a valuable, and, it is hoped, a permanent record of this interesting memorial of the aboriginal inhabitants of South-western Ontario.

The writer of this paper has been acquainted with "the old fort," as it was called, since the year 1867. At that time it was in the midst of the forest. Since then the woods have been cleared away, except within the fort and north of it. Indeed, a considerable number of trees have been felled within the southern part of the enclosure. In the mounds themselves trees are abundant, and there are many in the moat or ditch between. The stumps of those which have been cut down are so many chronological facts, from which the age of the fort may be con-

---

(a) Mr. J. H. Scott, of St. Thomas, has made a number of photographs of the mounds at the instance of an American lady, who, it is understood, will reproduce them in a work about to be published by her.

jectured with some approach to accuracy. A maple within the enclosure exhibits 242 rings of annual growth. It was probably the oldest tree within the walls. A maple in the outer embankment shows 197 rings; between the inner and outer walls a beech stump shows 219 rings, and an elm 266. Many of the trees were cut down a good many years ago. Judging from these stumps, it would be safe to calculate the age of the forest at about two hundred years, with here and there a tree a little older. The area enclosed is level. In the field south there are numerous hummocks formed by the decayed stumps of fallen trees. The walls were manifestly thrown up from the outside. There is an exception on the south-east. Here the ground outside was higher, and to get the requisite elevation the earth was thrown up on both walls from the intervening space, as well as on the exterior wall from the outside. Each of the walls runs completely round the enclosure, except where the steep bank of the little stream was utilized to eke out the inner wall for five or six rods on the west side, as shewn on the plan. Opposite the south end of this gap was the original entrance through the outer wall. The walls have been cut through in one or two other places, doubtless by settlers hauling timber across them.

The writer accompanied Mr. Campbell on his visits in the spring and fall of 1891. The members of the Elgin Historical and Scientific Institute made a pretty thorough examination of a large ash-heap south-east of the fort. It had, however, been frequently dug into during the last score or two of years, with ample results, it is said, in the way of stone implements of various kinds. There still remained, however, arrow-heads and chippings of flint, stones partially disintegrated from the action of heat, fragments of pottery whose markings showed a very low stage of artistic development, fish scales, charred maize and bones of small animals, the remains of aboriginal banquets. Within the enclosure, corn-cobs were found by digging down through the mould, and a good specimen of a bone needle, well smoothed, but without any decoration, was turned up in the bed of the little stream where it passes through the fort.

The original occupants were manifestly hunters, fishermen and agriculturists, as well as warriors. Nothing appears to have been found in the neighborhood, pointing to any intercourse between them and any European race.

It would seem that the earth-work was constructed in the midst of a large clearing, and that the forest grew up after the disappearance of the occupants. A few saplings, however, may have been permitted to spring up during their occupancy for the sake of the shelter they might afford. These are represented by the oldest stumps above mentioned.

The question, who were the builders, is an interesting one. To answer it we need not go back to a remoter period than the middle of the seventeenth century, when the Iroquois after destroying the Huron Settlements turned their attention to the southwest, and the Neutral Nation ceased to exist. The enclosure was, we may reasonably believe, a fortified village of the Neutrals at the time of their evacuation of this province, nearly a quarter of a millennium ago.

Substantially all that is known of the Neutrals is to be found in Champlain's works, Sagard's History, the Relations and Journal of the Jesuits, and Sanson's map of 1656. A digest of the information contained therein is given in the following pages. The writer has availed himself of one or two other works for some of the facts mentioned. Mr. Benjamin Sulte's interesting and learned articles on " Le pays des grands lacs au XVIIe Siecle" in that excellent magazine, "Le Canada Francais," have been most valuable in this connection.

The first recorded visit to the Neutrals was in the winter of 1626, by a Recollet father, De Laroche-Daillon. His experiences are narrated by himself, and Sagard, who includes the narrative in his history, supplements it with one or two additional facts.

In company with the Jesuit Fathers Brebeuf and De Noue, Daillon left Quebec with the purpose of visiting and converting the Hurons, who were settled in villages between the Georgian Bay and Lake Simcoe. After the usual hardships, journeying by canoe and portage, by way of the Ottawa and French Rivers, they arrived at their destination. The ill-fated Brule told wonderful stories of a nation, whom the French called the Neutrals, and Father Joseph Le Caron wrote Daillon urging him to continue his journey as far as their country.

He set out accordingly on the 18th October, 1626, with two

other Frenchmen, Grenolle and La Vallee. Passing through the territory occupied by the Tobacco Nation, he met one of their chiefs, who not merely offered his services as guide, but furnished Indian porters to carry their packs and their scanty provisions. They slept five nights in the woods, and on the sixth day arrived at the village of the Neutrals. In this as well as in four other villages which they visited, they were hospitably entertained with presents of food, including venison, pumpkins, "neintahouy," and "the best they had." Their dress excited the astonishment of their Indian hosts, who were also surprised that the missionary asked nothing from them but that they should raise their eyes to heaven, and make the sign of the cross.

What excited raptures of admiration, however, according to his narrative was to see him retire for prayer at certain hours of the day; for they had never seen any priests beyond passing glimpses when visiting amongst the neighboring Hurons and Tobacco Indians.

At the sixth village, Ounontisaston, in which Daillon had been advised to take up his abode, a council was held at his instance. He observes that the councils are called at the will of the chiefs, and held either in a wigwam or in the open air, the audience being seated on the ground; that silence is preserved whilst a chief is addressing the assembly, and that what they have once concluded and settled is inviolably observed and performed by them.

Daillon explained that he had come on the part of the French to make alliance and friendship with them and to invite them to come and trade, and begged them to permit him to stay in their country "to instruct them in the laws of our God, which is the only means of going to Paradise." They agreed to all he proposed and in return for his gifts of knives and other trifles, they adopted him as "citizen and child of the country," and as a mark of great affection entrusted him to the care of Souharissen, who became his father and host. The latter was, according to Daillon, the chief of the greatest renown and authority that had ever been known in all the nations, being chief not only of his own village, but of all those of his nation, to the number of twenty-eight, besides several little hamlets of seven to eight cabins built in different places convenient for fishing, hunting, or cultivating the ground. Souharissen had acquired his absolute and extraordinary authority by his courage and his success in war. He had been several times at war with the seventeen tribes, who were the enemies of his race, and from all he had brought back the heads of those he had slain, or prisoners taken alive, as tokens of his prowess. His authority was without example amongst other tribes.

The Neutrals are reported by Daillon as being very warlike, armed only with war-club and bow, and dexterous in their use. His companions having gone back, the missionary remained alone, "the happiest man in the world," seeking to advance the glory of God and to find the mouth of the river of the Iroquois, (probably the Niagara,) in order to conduct the savages to the French trading posts. He visited them in their huts, found them very manageable and learned their customs. He remarked that there were no deformed people amongst them. The children, who were sprightly, naked and unkempt, were taught by him to make the sign of the Holy Cross.

The natives were willing that at least four canoes should go to trade if he would conduct them, but nobody knew the way. Yroquet, an Indian known in the country, who had come hunting with twenty of his tribe and secured five hundred beaver skins, declined to give him any indication of the mouth of the river; but he agreed with several Hurons in assuring Daillon that a journey of ten days would take him to the trading post. The missionary, however, was afraid of taking one river for another and getting lost or perishing of hunger.

For three months he was treated with kindness. Then the Hurons became jealous lest the trade should be diverted from them. They accordingly circulated rumors through every village, that Daillon was a great magician, that he had poisoned the air in their country, and many had died in consequence, that if he was not killed soon, he would burn up their villages and kill their children, with other stories as extraordinary and alarming about the entire French nation. The Neutrals were easily influenced by the reports. Daillon's life was in danger on more than one occasion. The rumor reached Brebeuf and De Noue, that he had been killed. They at once despatched Grenolle to ascertain the truth, with instructions to bring Daillon back if alive. He acquiesced, and returned to the Huron country.

He speaks of a Neutral village called Ouaroronon, one day's journey from the Iroquois, the people of which came to trade at Ounontisaston. Their village was the last of the Neutral villages, and was probably east of the Niagara River.

Daillon, like every other traveller, was charmed with the Neutral country, which he pronounces incomparably greater, more beautiful and better than any other "of all these countries." He notes the incredible number of deer, the native mode of taking them by driving them into a gradually narrowing enclosure, their practice of killing every animal they find whether they needed it or not. The reason alleged was that if they did not kill all, the beasts that escaped would tell the others how they had been chased, so that afterwards when the Indians needed game it would be impossible to get near it. He enumerates moose, beaver, wild-cats, squirrels larger than those of France, bustards, turkeys, cranes, etc., as abundant, and remaining in the country through the winter. The winter was shorter and milder than "in Canada." No snow had fallen by the 22nd November. The deepest was not more than two and a half feet. Thaw set in on the 26th of January. On the 8th March the snow was gone from the open places, but a little still lingered in the woods. The streams abounded in very good fish. The ground produced more corn than was needed, besides pumpkins, beans and other vegetables in abundance, and excellent oil. He expresses his surprise that the Merchants' Company had not sent some Frenchman to winter in the Country; for it would be very easy to get the Neutrals to trade and the direct route would be much shorter than that by way of French River and the Georgian Bay. He describes the Neutrals' country as being nearer than the Huron to the French, and as being on one side of the lake of the Iroquois (Lake Ontario) whilst the Iroquois were on the other. The Neutrals, however, did not understand the management of canoes, especially in the rapids, of which there were only two, but long and dangerous. Their proper trade was hunting and war. They were very lazy and immoral. Their manners and customs were very much the same as those of the Hurons. Their language was different, but the members of the two nations understood one another. They went entirely unclad.

Sagard adds that "according to the opinion of some," the

Neutrals' country was eighty leagues (about 200 miles) in extent, and that they raised very good tobacco which they traded with their neighbors. They were called Neutrals on account of their neutrality between the Hurons and the Iroquois; but they were allies of the Cheveux Releves (the Ottawas) against their mortal enemies of the Nation of Fire. Sagard was dissuaded by some members of the French trading company from attempting to bring about a peace between the Hurons and the Iroquois. It was supposed that this would divert the trade of the Hurons from Quebec by sending it through the Iroquois country to the Dutch of the Hudson River. At so early a date did the question of closer trade relations between the territories north and south of the lakes agitate the minds of statesmen and men of commerce.

In the winter of 1640-1, the Jesuit missionaries, Brebeuf and Chaumonot traversed the country of the Neutrals. The former composed a dictionary showing the differences between the kindred dialects of the Hurons and Neutrals. Chaumonot made a map of the country, which is not extant, but there is reason for believing that it was the authority for the delineation of the territory on Sanson's map of 1656 and Ducreux's Latin map of 1660. From the facts hereinafter detailed it is highly probable that they reached the Detroit River, and that they visited and named the Neutral village of which the Southwold Earthwork is the memorial. The first printed map in which Lake Erie is shown was made by N. Sanson d'Abbeville, geographer in ordinary to the King, and printed in Paris, with "privilege du Roy" for twenty years, in the year 1656. It is a map of eastern North America. The sources of information are stated in general terms, which may be translated as follows: "The most northerly portion is drawn from the various Relations "of the English, Danes, etc. Towards the south the coasts of "Virginia, New Sweden, New Netherlands and New England "are drawn from those of the English, Dutch, etc. THE GREAT "RIVER OF CANADA, or of St. Lawrence and all the neighboring "regions (*environs*) are according to the Relations of the French."

Now, we know that Father Raymbault visited Sault Ste. Marie in 1641 and mapped Lake Superior, and that Father Chaumonot in the same year rendered the same service for the

Neutral Country. Sanson's map is fairly accurate for the upper lakes, when compared with some maps published at much later periods when the lakes had become tolerably well known to traders and travellers. It shows an acquaintance with the general contour of Lakes Erie, St. Clair and Huron, with several of the streams emptying into Lakes Erie and Huron on both the Canadian and the American sides, with the names of tribes inhabiting both shores, and with the locations of five towns of the Neutrals, besides some towns of the Tobacco Nation. The Neutral towns are given as S. Francois, (north-east of Sarnia) S. Michel, (a little east of Sandwich), S. Joseph, (apparently in the county of Kent), Alexis, (a few miles west of a stream, which flows into Lake Erie about midway between the Detroit and Niagara Rivers, and where the shore bends farthest inland), (*b*) and N. D. des Anges (on the West bank of a considerable river, probably the Grand River, near where Brantford now stands). The Detroit and Niagara Rivers and four streams flowing into Lake Erie between them are shown but not named. The great cataract is called "Ongiara Sault." The name Ongiara may, however, be that of the Neutral village east of the Falls. Lake St. Clair is called Lac des Eaux de Mer, or Sea-water Lake, possibly from the mineral springs in the neighborhood. The country of the Tobacco Nation includes the Bruce peninsula and extends from the Huron country on the east to Lake Huron on the west, and Burlington Bay on the southeast. The Neutral Country (*Neutre ou Attiouandarons*) would embrace the whole of southwestern Ontario south of a line drawn from the west end of Lake Ontario to a stream which flows into Lake Huron about midway between Point Edward and Cape Hurd, and which is probably the Maitland River. The tribes to the south of the lakes are indicated from the Niagara River to Lake Superior. The Eries or "Eriechronons, ou du Chat," are south-east of Lake Erie; the 'Ontarraronon" are west of what is probably the Cuyahoga River; at the southwest of the lake appear the "Squenqioronon;" west of the Detroit River are the "Aictaeronon;" west of Port Huron the "Couarronon;" Huron County in

---

(*b*) Alexis corresponds with the actual position of the Southwold Earthwork, and the stream with that of Kettle Creek.

THE COUNTRY OF THE NEUTRALS. 9

▓ichigan is occupied by the "Ariaetoeronon;" at the head of
▓ginaw Bay and extending southward through Michigan are
▓ istaeronons ou du Feu;" in the peninsula extending
▓ ▓c are the "Oukouarararonons;" beyond them
▓ as "Lac de Puans;" then come the
nort▓ ▓uperieur." Manitoulin Island is
marked ▓ the old French name for the
Ottawas. The ▓tion called "N. du Petun on
Sanhionontatehcronons" ▓cludes villages of "S. Simon et S.
Iude" in the Bruce promontory, "S. Pierre" near the south end
of the County of Bruce, and "S. Pol," southwest of a lake which
may be Scugog.

To return to the narratives, these agree in stating
that the Neutrals, like their kinsmen of the Huron, Tobacco
and Iroquois Nations, were a numerous and sedentary race
living in villages and cultivating their fields of maize,
tobacco and pumpkins. They were on friendly terms with the
eastern and northern tribes, but at enmity with those of the
west, especially the Nation of Fire, against whom they were
constantly sending out war parties. By the western tribes it
would appear that those west of the Detroit River and Lake
Huron are invariably meant.

Champlain refers to the Neutrals in 1616 as a powerful
nation, holding a large extent of country, and numbering 4,000
warriors. Already they were in alliance with the Cheveux
Releves (the Ottawas), whom he visited in the Bruce Peninsula,
against the Nation of Fire. He states that the Neutrals lived
two days' journey southward of the Cheveux Releves, and the
Nation of Fire ten days from the latter. The Nation of Fire
occupied part of what is now Michigan, probably as far east
as the Detroit and St. Clair Rivers.

Describing his visit to the Cheveux Releves, he adds:—"I had
"a great desire to go and see that Nation (the Neutrals), had not
"the tribes where we were dissuaded me from it, saying that
"the year before one of ours had killed one of them, being at war
"with the Entouhoronons (the Senecas), and that they were
"angry on account of it, representing to us that they are very
"subject to vengeance, not looking to those who dealt the blow,
"but the first whom they meet of the nation, or even their

"friends, they make them bear the penalty, when they can catch
"any of them unless beforehand peace had been made with the
"and one had given them some gifts and presen
"relatives of the deceased; which prevented
"from going there, although some of th
"they would do us no harm for s, and
"occasioned our returning by the s come, and
"continuing my journey, I found th of the Pisierinij etc."

Brebeuf, who reckoned the Hurons at more than 30,000, describes the Neutrals in 1634 as much more numerous than the former. The Relation of 1641 gives them at least 12,000, but adds that notwithstanding the wars, famine and disease (small pox), which since three years had prevailed in an extraordinary degree, the country could still furnish 4,000 warriors, the exact number estimated by Champlain a quarter of a century earlier. The name of the Neutrals is variously given as Attikadaron, Atiouandaronk, Attiouandaron, Attiwandaronk, but the last is the more common. The name signified "people who spoke a slightly different dialect," and the Hurons were known to the Neutrals by the same name. The latter are mentioned in the Relations as one of the twelve numerous and sedentary nations who spoke a common language with the Hurons. The Oueanohronons formed "one of the nations associated with the Neutral Nation." They are afterwards called in the same Relation (1639) the Wenrohronons, and are said to have lived on the borders of the Iroquois, more than eighty leagues from the Huron country. So long as they were on friendly terms with the Neutrals they were safe from the dreaded Iroquois; but a misunderstanding having arisen between them, they were obliged to flee in order to avoid extermination by the latter. They took refuge, more than 600 in all, with the Hurons, and were received in the most friendly and hospitable manner.

The Relation of 1640 speaks of a Huron map communicated by Father Paul Ragueneau in which a large number of tribes, most of them acquainted with the Huron language, are shown, including the Iroquois, the Neutrals, the Eries, etc. The "Mission of the Apostles" was established among the Tobacco

---

NOTE.—This is a literal translation, and shows the crudity of Champlain's sailor style of composition.

Nation by Garnier and Jogues in 1640. Nine villages visited by them were endowed by the missionaries with the names of apostles, two of which are given in Sanson's map of 1656. (c) In one "bourg" called S. Thomas, they baptized a boy five years old belonging to the Neutral Nation, who died immediately afterwards. "He saw himself straightway out of banishment and happy in his own country." The famine had driven his parents to the village of the Tobacco Nation. The devoted missionaries add, that this was the first fruits of the Neutral nation.

In the fall of the same year "The Mission of the Angels" was begun among the Neutrals. The lot fell upon Jean de Brebeuf and Joseph Marie Chaumonot. The former was the pioneer of the Jesuit Mission. He had spent three years among the Hurons from 1626 to 1629, and, after the restoration of Canada to the French by Charles I., he had returned in 1634 to the scene of his earlier labors. His associate had only come from France the year before. Brebeuf was distinguished for his mastery of the native tongues, and Chaumonot had been recognized as an apt student of languages. The plan of the Jesuits was to establish in the new mission a fixed and permanent residence, which should be the "retreat" of the missionaries of the surrounding country, as Ste. Marie was of those of the Huron mission.

Lalemant from their report describes the Neutral Nation as exceedingly populous, including about forty villages ("bourgs ou bourgades.") The nearest villages were four or five days' journey or about forty leagues (100 miles) distant from the Hurons, going due south. He estimates the difference in latitude between Ste. Marie and the nearest village of the Neutrals to the south at about 1°55'. Elsewhere the distance is spoken of as about thirty leagues.

From the first "bourg," going on to the south or south-west (a mistake for south-east it would seem,) it was about four days' journey to the mouth of the Niagara River. On this side of the

---

(c) The principal "bourg" was Ehwae, surnamed S. Pierre et S. Paul. If S. Pierre on Sanson's map is the same place, this must have been near the southern end of the county of Bruce. The other village or mission shown on the map is S. Simon et S Iude.

river, and not beyond it, as "some map" lays it down, (Champlain's, doubtless,) were most of the "bourgs" of the Neutral Nation. There were three or four on the other side towards the Eries. Lalemant claims, and there is no doubt as to the fact, that the French were the first Europeans to become acquainted with the Neutrals. The Hurons and Iroquois were sworn enemies to each other, but in a wigwam or even a camp of the Neutrals until recently each had been safe from the other's vengeance.

Latterly however the unbridled fury of the hostile nations had not respected even the neutral ground of their mutual friends. Friendly as they were to the Hurons and Iroquois, the Neutrals engaged in cruel wars with other nations to the west, particularly the Nation of Fire, as has been stated above. The previous year a hundred prisoners had been taken from the latter tribe. This year, returning with 2,000 warriors, the Neutrals had carried off more than 170. Fiercer than the Hurons, they burned their female prisoners. Their clothing and mode of living differed but little from those of the Hurons. They had Indian corn, beans and pumpkins in equal abundance. Fish were abundant, different species being met with in different places. The country was a famous hunting ground. Elk, deer, wild cats, wolves, "black beasts" (squirrels) beaver and other animals valuable for their skins and flesh, were in abundance. It was a rare thing to see more than half a foot of snow. This year there was more than three feet. The deep snow had facilitated the hunting, and, in happy contrast with the famine which had prevailed, meat was plentiful. They had also multitudes of wild turkeys which went in flocks through the fields and woods. Fruits were no more plentiful than amongst the Hurons, except that chestnuts abounded, and wild apples were a little larger.

Their manners and customs, and family and political government, were very much like those of the other Indian tribes. but they were distinguished from the Hurons by their greater dissoluteness and indecency. On the other hand they were taller, stronger and better formed.

Their burial customs were peculiar, although similar customs are reported at this day amongst some African tribes. The bodies remained in their wigwams until decomposition rendered them insupportable, when they were put outside on a scaffold. Soon afterward, the bones were removed and arranged within their houses on both sides in sight of the inmates, where they remained until the feast of the dead. Having these mournful objects before their eyes, the women habitually indulged in cries and laments, in a kind of chant.

The Neutrals were distinguished for the multitude and quality of their madmen, who were a privileged class. Hence it was common for bad Indians to assume the character of maniacs in order to perpetrate crimes without fear of punishment. The Jesuits suffered very much from their malice. Some old men told them that the Neutrals used to carry on war "towards" a certain western nation, who would seem to have lived on the Gulf of Mexico, where the "porcelain, which are the pearls of the country," was obtained from a kind of oysters. It is an undoubted fact that a traffic was carried on with tribes as far south as the Gulf of Mexico, from whom shells used for wampum were obtained by successive interchanges of commodities with intervening tribes. They had also some vague notion of alligators, which are apparently referred to by the description, "certain aquatic animals, larger and swifter than elk," against which these same people had "a kind of war," the details of which are somewhat amusing, as given by Lalemant.

The two Jesuits left Ste. Marie the 2nd November, 1640, with two French servants (probably "donnes,") and an Indian. They slept four nights in the woods. The fifth day they arrived at the first village ("bourg") of the Neutral Nation called Kandoucho, but to which they gave the name of All Saints. This is probably the same as N. D. des Anges on Sanson's map, and was not far perhaps from the site of Brantford.

Owing to the unfavorable reports which had been spread through the country about the Jesuits, the latter were anxious to explain their purposes to a council of the chiefs and old men. The head chief, "who managed the affairs of the public" was called Tsohahissen (doubtless the same as Daillon's Souharissen). His "bourg" was "in the middle of the country;" to reach it, one had to pass through several other villages ("bourgs et bourgades.") In Sanson's map, Alexis is placed almost exactly "in the middle of the country" of the Neutrals. No other village is marked on the map, to which the expression could be applied. Its situation nearly midway between the Detroit & Niagara Rivers, a few miles west of a stream which flows into Lake Erie just where the mouth of Kettle Creek would appear in a map of our own century, corresponds with that of the Southwold earthwork. Was the latter the Neutrals' capital? We can only conjecture; but the evidence of the Relations, the map and the forest growth, all points to an affirmative answer. There is a strong probability that it was here Tsohahissen reigned (if the expression is allowable in reference to an Indian potentate) as head chief of the forty Neutral villages. Through the western gate, doubtless, his warriors set out to wage their relentless warfare against the Nation of Fire. Within these mounds, returning satiated with blood, they celebrated their savage triumph, adorned with the scalps of their enemies.

Brebeuf's Huron surname "Echon" had preceded him. He was regarded as "one of the most famous sorcerers and demons "ever imagined." Several Frenchmen had travelled through the country before him, purchasing furs and other commodities. These had smoothed the way for the Jesuits. Under the pretext of being traders, Brebeuf's party succeeded in making their way in spite of all obstacles interposed. They arrived at the head-chief's village, only to find that he had gone on a war party and would not return until spring. The missionaries sought to negotiate with those who administered affairs in his absence. They desired to publish the Gospel throughout these lands, "and "thereby to contract a particular alliance with them." In proof of their desire, they had brought a necklace of two thousand grains of "porcelain" or wampum which they wished to present to "the Public." The inferior chiefs refused to bind themselves in any way by accepting the present, but gave the missionaries leave, if they would wait until the chief of the country returned, to travel freely and give such instruction as they pleased. Nothing could have suited the fathers better. First however they decided to return in their steps and reconduct their domestics out of the country. Then they would resume their journey for the second time, and "begin their function." As it had been the servants however, who had acted the part of traders, this pretext was now wanting to the Jesuits. They suffered everywhere from the malicious reports which had been circulated as to their purposes in visiting the nation and the acts of sorcery with which they were charged. The Hurons of the Georgian Bay alarmed for the monopoly they had hitherto enjoyed and jealous of the French traders, had sent emissaries amongst the Neutrals to poison their minds against the adventurous travellers, by the most extraordinary calumnies.

For these reports two Huron Indians Aouenhokoui and Oentara were especially responsible. They had visited several villages, presented hatchets in the name of the Huron chiefs and old men, and denounced their white visitors as sorcerers who desired to destroy the Neutrals by means of presents. These representations were so effectual that a council was at length held by the chiefs and the present formally refused, although permission to preach was granted.

From village to village they passed, but everywhere the doors were barred to them. Hostile looks greeted them wherever they went. No sooner did they approach a village than the cry resounded on all sides "Here come the Agwa." This was the name given by the natives to their greatest enemies. If the priests were admitted into their dwellings at all, it was more frequently from fear of the " sorcerers'" vengeance than for the hope of gain, "God making use of everything in order to nourish his servants."

In the graphic language of Lalemant: "The mere sight of the fathers, in figure and habit so different from their own, their gait, their gestures and their whole deportment seemed to them so many confirmations of what had been told them. The breviaries, ink-stands and writings were instruments of magic; if the Frenchmen prayed to God, it was according to their idea simply an exercise of sorcerers. Going to the stream to wash their dishes, it was said they were poisoning the water: it was charged that through all the cabins, wherever the priests passed, the children were seized with a cough and bloody flux, and the women became barren. In short, there was no calamity present or to come, of which they were not considered as the source. Several of those with whom the fathers took up their abode did not sleep day or night for fear; they dared not touch what had been handled by them, they returned the strangers' presents, regarding everything as suspicious. The good old women already regarded themselves as lost, and only regretted the fate of their little children, who might otherwise have been able to repeople the earth."

The Neutrals intimidated the fathers with rumors of the Senecas, who they were assured were not far off. They spoke of killing and eating the missionaries. Yet in the four months of their sojourn Brebeuf and Chaumonot never lacked the necessaries of life, lodging and food, and amidst difficulties and inconveniences better imagined than described they retained their health. Their food supply was bread baked under ashes after the fashion of the country, and which they kept for thirty and even forty days to use in case of need.

"In their journey, the fathers passed through eighteen "villages (*bourgs ou bourgades*), to all of which they gave a "Christian name, of which we shall make use hereafter on "occasion. They stayed particularly in ten, to which they gave "as much instruction as they could find hearers. They report "about 500 Fires and 3,000 persons, which these ten *bourgades* "may contain, to whom they set forth and published the Gospel." (Lalemant's Relation.) (*d*)

Disheartened, the fathers decided to return to Kandoucho or All Saints to await the spring. Midway, however, at the village of Teotongniaton, or S. Guillaume, (perhaps in the vicinity of Woodstock) the snow fell in such quantities that further progress was impossible. They lodged here in the cabin of a squaw, who entertained them hospitably and instructed them in the language, dictating narratives syllable by syllable as to a school boy. Here they stayed twenty-five days, "adjusted the dictionary and "rules of the Huron language to that of these tribes (the "Neutrals), and accomplished a work which alone was worth a "journey of several years in the country."

Hurons from the mission of La Conception volunteered to go to the relief of the daring travellers. After eight days of travel and fatigue in the woods the priests and the relief party arrived at Ste. Marie on the very day of St. Joseph, patron of the country, in time to say mass, which they had not been able

---

(*d*) In another place it is stated that there were 40 villages of the Neutrals in all.

to say since their departure.

Amongst the eighteen villages visited by them, only one, that of Khioetoa, called by the fathers Saint Michel, gave them the audience their embassy merited. In this village, years before, driven by fear of their enemies, had taken refuge a certain foreign nation, " which lived beyond Erie or the Cat "Nation," named Aouenrehronon. It was in this nation that the fathers performed the first baptism of adults. These were probably a portion of the kindred Neutral tribe referred to above as having fled to the Huron country from the Iroquois. Their original home was in the State of New York. Sanson's map shows S. Michel a little east of where Sandwich now stands.

Owing to their scanty number and the calumnies circulated amongst the Indians respecting the Jesuits of the Huron Mission the latter resolved to concentrate their forces. The Neutral mission was abandoned, but Christian Indians visited the Neutrals in 1643 and spread the faith amongst them with a success which elicits Lalemant's enthusiastic praises. Towards the end of the following winter a band of about 500 Neutrals visited the Hurons. The fathers did not fail to avail themselves of their opportunity. The visitors were instructed in the faith and expressed their regret that their teachers could not return with them. A different reception from that experienced by Brebeuf and Chaumonot three years before was promised.

Lalemant relates that in the summer of 1643, 2,000 Neutrals invaded the country of the Nation of Fire and attacked a village strongly fortified with a palissade, and defended stoutly by 900 warriors. After a ten days' siege, they carried it by storm, killed a large number on the spot, and carried off 800 captives, men women and children, after burning 70 of the most warlike and blinding the eyes and "girdling the mouths" of the old men, whom they left to drag out a miserable existence. He reports the Nation of Fire as more populous than the Neutrals, the Hurons and the Iroquois together. In a large number of these villages the Algonkin language was spoken. Farther away, it was the prevailing tongue. In remote Algonkin tribes, even at that early day, there were Christians who knelt, crossed their hands, turned their eyes heavenward, and prayed to God morning and evening, and before and after their meals; and the best mark of their faith was that they were no longer wicked nor dishonest as they were before. So it was reported to Lalemant by trustworthy Hurons who went every year to trade with Algonkin nations scattered over the whole northern part of the continent.

Ragueneau in the Relation of 1648 refers to Lake Erie as being almost 200 leagues in circuit, and precipitating itself by "a "waterfall of a terrible height" into Lake Ontario, or Lake Saint Louys.

The Aondironnons a tribe of the Neutrals living nearest to the Hurons were treacherously attacked in their village by 300 Senecas, who after killing a number carried as many as possible away with them as prisoners. The Neutrals showed no open resentment but quietly prepared to revenge themselves. A Christian Huron, a girl of fifteen, taken prisoner by the Senecas, escaped from them and made her way to the Neutral country, where she met four men, two of whom were Neutrals and the others enemies. The latter wished to take her back to captivity; but the Neutrals, claiming that within their country she was no longer in the power of her enemies, rescued her and she returned in safety to Ste. Marie on the Georgian Bay. These incidents were the prelude to the storm which shortly afterward burst.

In 1650 the principal part of the Iroquois forces was directed against the Neutrals. They carried two frontier villages, in one of which were more than 1600 men, the first at the end of autumn, the second early in the spring of 1651. The old men and children who might encumber them on their homeward journey were massacred. The number of captives was excessive, especially of young women, who were carried off to the Iroquois towns. The other more distant villages were seized with terror. The Neutrals abandoned their houses, their property and their country. Famine pursued them. The survivors became scattered amongst far-off woods and along unknown lakes and rivers. In wretchedness and want and in constant apprehension of their relentless enemy, they eked out a miserable existence.

The Journal (April 22, 1651) adds that after the destruction of the Neutral village in the previous autumn, the Neutral warriors under the lead of the Tahontaenrat (a Huron tribe) had followed the assailants and killed or taken 200 of them; and 1,200 Iroquois warriors had returned in the spring to avenge this disaster. In August a Huron reported at Montreal the capture of Teot'ondiaton (probably the village in which Brebeuf composed his dictionary, and which is referred to in the Relation as having been taken in the spring). The condition of the Neutrals was desolate and desperate. In April, 1652, news reached Quebec that they had leagued with the Andastes against the Iroquois, that the Senecas had been defeated in a foray against the Neutrals, so that the Seneca women had been constrained to quit their village and retreat to the Oneida country; also that the Mohawks had gone on the war path against the Andastes during the winter, and the issue of the war was unknown. The last of July, 1653, seven Indians from the Huron country arrived at Quebec and reported a great gathering near Mackinac of all the Algonkin nations with the remains of the Tobacco and Neutral Nations at A,otonatendie three days above the Sault Ste. Marie (Skia,e) towards the south. The Tobacco Indians had wintered at Tea,onto'rai; the Neutrals to the number of 800 at Sken'chio,e towards Teo'chanontian. These were to rendezvous the next fall with the Algonkins, who were already on the spot to the number of 1,000.

This is probably the last we hear of the Neutrals under their own name. Some of the survivors united with the remnant of the Hurons at Mackinac and on Lake Superior; and under the name of the Hurons and Wyandots they appear from time to time on the page of history. Their removal to Detroit on the establishment of the latter trading post by Cadaillac, is perpetuated by the name of Wyandotte, to the south of the City of the Straits.

Parkman mentions the circumstance that an old chief named Kenjockety, who claimed descent from an adopted prisoner of the Neutral Nation, was recently living among the Senecas of Western New York.

It is stated in the "History of the County of Middlesex" that over 60 years ago, "Edouard Petit, of Black River, discovered the ruins of an ancient building on the Riviere aux Sables, about 40 miles from Sarnia. Pacing the size, he found it to have been 40x24 feet on the ground. On the middle of the south or gable end, was a chimney eighteen feet high, in excellent preservation, built of stone, with an open fire place. The fire place had sunk below the surface. This ruin had a garden surrounding it, ten or twelve rods wide by twenty rods in length, marked by ditches and alleys. Inside the walls of the house a splendid oak had grown to be three feet in diameter, with a stem sixty feet high to the first branch. It seemed to be of second growth, and must have been 150 years reaching its proportions as seen in 1828-9."

This must have been the mission of S. Francois shown on Sanson's map.

THE IROQUOIS' HUNTING GROUND.

After the expulsion of the Neutrals, the north shore of Lake Erie remained an unpeopled wilderness until the close of the last century. The unbroken forest teemed with deer, racoons, foxes, wolves, bears, squirrels and wild turkeys. Millions of pigeons darkened the sky in their seasons of migration. For generations after the disappearance of the Neutrals, the Iroquois resorted to the region in pursuit of game. The country was described in maps as "*Chasse de Castor des Iroquois*," the Iroquois' beaver ground. Numerous dams constructed by these industrious little animals still remain to justify the description.

The French built forts at Detroit, Niagara and Toronto to intercept the beaver traffic, which otherwise might be shared by the English on the Hudson and Mohawk rivers; but for nearly a hundred and fifty years no settlement was attempted on the north shore. References to the region are few and scanty. Travellers did not penetrate into the country. Coasting along the shore in canoes on their way to Detroit, they landed as rarely as possible for shelter or repose. There were forest paths well known to the Indians, by which they portaged their canoes and goods from one water stretch to another. One of these led from the site of Dundas to a point on the Grand River near Cainsville; another from the latter stream to the Thames River near Woodstock; and a third from the upper waters of the Thames to Lake Huron. Besides these, there was a trail from the Huntly farm in Southwold on the River Thames (Lot 11,

Con. 1,) to the mouth of Kettle Creek; and a fifth from the Rondeau to M'Gregor's Creek near Chatham. These were thoroughfares of travel and of such rude commerce as was carried on by the savages with their French and English neighbors.

THE FRENCH EXPLORATION.

Joliet was the first Frenchman to descend Lake Erie from Detroit. He had been sent by Talon to investigate the copper mines of Lake Superior. He returned to Quebec in the autumn of 1669 by way of the lower lakes, instead of taking the usual route by the French River and the Ottawa. At the mouth of Kettle Creek he hid his canoe. Thence he portaged, doubtless by the well-known trails to the Thames and Grand rivers, until he reached Burlington Bay. (*e*).

At the Seneca village of Tinaouatoua, midway between the Bay and the Grand River, he met La Salle and the Sulpician priests, Dollier de Casson and Galinee on their way to Lake Erie and the Ohio River. The result of the meeting and of the information given by Joliet was that the priests altered their purpose and decided to proceed to Sault Ste. Marie and then to the Pottamatamies, where they would establish their mission: whilst La Salle, who evidently was dissatisfied with his companions, went back with Joliet and, it is now pretty generally believed, discovered the Ohio by journeying overland from the Seneca villages south of Lake Ontario during the winter or the following spring. Joliet gave the missionaries a description of his route, from which Galinee was able to make a map which was of great assistance in the further progress of their expedition. (*f*). The priests descended the Grand River to Lake Erie, and wintered at the forks of Patterson's Creek, where Port Dover now stands. After a sojourn of five months and eleven days, during which they were visited in their cabin by Iroquois beaver hunters, they proceeded westward along the north shore of the lake. Losing one of their canoes in a storm, they were obliged to divide their party. Four men with the luggage proceeded in the two remaining canoes. Five of the party, including apparently the two priests, made the wearisome

---
(*e*) This is the most probable inference from the facts stated by Galinee.
(*f*) Galinee's map is reproduced in Faillon's Histoire de la Colonie Francaise.

journey on foot from Long Point all the way to the mouth of Kettle Creek, where on the tenth of April, 1670, they found Joliet's canoe, and the party was reunited for the rest of the long journey to the Sault. Upon leaving their winter abode however the whole party had first proceeded to the lake shore, and there on the 23rd March 1670, being Passion Sunday, planted a cross, as a memorial of their long sojourn, and offered a prayer. The official record is as follows:

"We the undersigned certify that we have seen affixed on the "lands of the lake called Erie the arms of the King of France "with this inscription: The year of salvation 1669, Clement "IX. being seated in St. Peter's chair, Louis XIV. reigning in "France, M. de Courcelle being governor of New France, and "M. Talon being intendant therein for the King, there arrived in "this place two missionaries from Montreal accompanied by seven "other Frenchmen, who, the first of all European peoples, have "wintered on this lake, of which, as of a territory not occupied, "they have taken possession in the name of their King by the "apposition of his arms, which they have attached to the foot of "this cross. In witness whereof we have signed the present "certificate."

"FRANCOIS DOLLIER,
"Priest of the Diocese of Nantes in Brittany.
"DE GALINEE,
"Deacon of the Diocese of Rennes in Brittany."

Galinee grows enthusiastic over the abundance of game and wild fruits opposite Long Point. The grapes were as large and as sweet as the finest in France. The wine made from them was as good as *vin de grave*. He admires the profusion of walnuts, chestnuts, wild apples and plums. Bears were fatter and better to the palate than the most "savory" pigs in France. Deer wandered in herds of 50 to 100. Sometimes even 200 would be seen feeding together. In his enthusiasm the good priest calls this region "the terrestrial paradise of Canada."

Fortunately for the explorers, the winter was as mild at Port Dover as it was severe at Montreal. Patterson's Creek was however still frozen over on the 26th March, when, having portaged their goods and canoes to the lake, they embarked to resume their westward journey. They had to pass two streams before they arrived at the sand beach which connected Long Point with the mainland. To effect the first crossing they walked four leagues inland before they found a satisfactory spot. To cross Big Creek, they were obliged to spend a whole day constructing a raft. They were further delayed by a prolonged snow storm and a strong north wind. On the west bank was a meadow more than 200 paces wide, in passing over which they were immersed to their girdles in mud and slush. Arriving at the sandy ridge which then connected Long Point with the mainland, they found the lake on the other side full of floating ice, and concluded that their companions had not ventured to proceed in their frail barques. They encamped near the sandbar and waited for the canoes, which had doubtless been delayed by the weather. The missionaries put themselves on short rations in order to permit the hunters to keep up their strength for the chase, and were rewarded with a stag as the result. As it was Holy Week the whole party decided not to leave the spot until they had kept their Easter together. On the Tuesday following, which was the eighth day of April, they heard mass and, although the lake had still a border of ice, they launched their canoe, and continued their journey as before, five of the party going by land. When they arrived at "the place of the canoe," on the 10th great was their disappointment to find that the Iroquois had anticipated them and carried it away. Later in the day however it was found, hidden between two large trees on the other side of a stream. The discoverers came upon it unexpectedly whilst looking for dry wood to make a fire, and bore it in triumph to the lake. The hunters were out the whole day without seeing any game. For five or six days the party subsisted on boiled maize, no meat being obtainable. Being provided now with three canoes, the party paddled up the lake in one day to a place where game was abundant. The hunters saw more than 200 deer in a single herd, but missed their aim. In their craving for flesh-meat, they shot and skinned a poor wolf and had it ready for the kettle, when one of their men perceived twenty or thirty deer "on the other side "of a small lake on the shore of which we were." (*g*) The deer

---

(*g*) Evidently the Rondeau.

were surrounded and forced into the water, where 10 were killed, the rest being permitted to escape. Well supplied with fresh and smoked meat they went on nearly twenty leagues (about fifty miles) in one day, "as far as a long point which you will "find marked in the map of Lake Erie. We arrived there on a "beautiful sand-beach on the east side of this point." (*h*) Here disaster overtook them. They had drawn up their canoes beyond high water mark, but left their goods on the sand near the water, whilst they camped for the night. A terrific gale came up from the north-east, and the water of the lake rose until it swept with violence over the beach. One of the party was awakened by the roaring of the waves and wind and aroused the rest, who attempted to save their supplies. Groping with torches along the shore, they succeeded in securing the cargo of Galinee's canoe, and of one of Dollier's. The other canoe load was lost, including provisions, goods for bartering, ammunition, and, most important of all, the altar service, with which they intended establishing their mission among the Pottawatamies. The question was debated whether they should take up their mission with some other tribe, or go back to Montreal for a new altar service and supplies, and, returning at a later period, establish themselves wherever they should then determine. Deciding in favor of the latter view, they concluded that the return journey would be as short by way of the Sault and the French River as by the route which they had followed from the east. In favor of this decision was the further consideration that not only would they see a new country but they would have the escort of the Ottawas who were assembling at the Sault for their annual trading visit to Montreal and Quebec. Galinee continues: "We pursued our journey accordingly towards the "west, and after having made about 100 leagues on Lake Erie "arrived at the place where the *Lake of the Hurons*, otherwise "called the *Fresh-water Sea of the Hurons*, or the Michigan, dis-"charges itself into that lake. This outlet is perhaps half a "league wide and turns sharply to the north-east, so that we "were in a measure retracing our steps; at the end of six leagues "we found a place that was very remarkable and held in great

---

(*h*) This was Point Pelee.

"veneration by all the savages of these regions, because of a
"stone idol of natural formation, to which they say they owe
"the success of their navigation on Lake Erie when they have
"crossed it without accident, and which they appease by
"sacrifices, presents of skins, provisions, etc., when they wish to
"embark on it."

"This place was full of huts of those who had come to pay
"homage to this idol, which had no other resemblance to a
"human figure than that which the imagination chose to give it.
"However it was painted all over, and a kind of face had been
"formed for it with vermillion. I leave you to imagine whether
"we avenged upon this idol, which the Iroquois had strongly
"recommended us to honor, the loss of our chapel."

"We attributed to it even the scarcity of food from which
"we had suffered up to that time. In fine there was nobody
"whose hatred it had not incurred. I consecrated one of my
"hatchets to break this god of stone, and then having locked
"canoes we carried the largest piece to the middle of the river,
"and immediately cast the remainder into the water, that it
"might never be heard of again."

"God rewarded us forthwith for this good act: for we killed
"a deer that same day, and four leagues farther we entered a
"little lake about ten leagues long and almost as wide, called by
"Mr. Sanson the *Lake of the Salted Waters*, but we saw no sign
"of salt. From this lake we entered the outlet of Lake
"Michigan, which is not a quarter of a league in width."

"At last ten or twelve leagues farther on, we entered the
"largest lake in all America, called here "the Fresh-water Sea
"of the Hurons," or in Algonkin, *Michigan*. It is 600 to 700
"leagues in circuit. We made on this lake 200 leagues and were
"afraid of falling short of provisions, the shores of the lake
"being apparently very barren. God, however, did not wish
"that we should lack for food in his service."

"For we were never more than one day without food. It is
"true that several times we had nothing left, and had to pass an
"evening and morning without having anything to put into the
"kettle, but I did not see that any one was discouraged or put to
"prayers (*sic*) on that account. For we were so accustomed to
"see that God succored us mightily in emergencies, that we

"awaited with tranquility the effects of his goodness, thinking
"that He who nourished so many barbarians in these woods
"would not abandon his servants."

"We passed this lake without any peril and entered the *Lake
"of the Hurons*, which communicates with it by four mouths,
"each nearly two leagues in width."

"At last we arrived on the 25th May, the day of Pentecost,
"at Ste. Marie of the Sault, where the Jesuit fathers have made
"their principal establishment for the missions to the Ottawas
"and neighboring tribes."

Here they found fathers D'Ablon and Marquette in charge of the mission, with a fort consisting of a square of cedar posts, enclosing a chapel and residence. They had cleared and seeded a large piece of ground. The Sulpicians remained only three days and then hired an experienced guide to take them to Montreal, where they arrived on the 18th June after a fatiguing journey of twenty-two days. They had been absent since the 6th July 1669, and were welcomed as if they had come to life again after being dead. It was their intention to return in the following spring and renew their search for the Ohio River, where they purposed establishing a mission; but this intention was never carried into effect.

"This famous voyage," says Dean Harris in his interesting "'History of the Early Missions in Western Canada,' stimulated "to an extraordinary degree enthusiasm for discovery, and in "the following year Talon sent out expeditions to the Hudson "Bay, the Southern Sea, and into the Algonquin country to the "north." Marquette, Tonty, Hennepin, Du Lhut, La Salle and Perrot explored the Mississippi valley, and the head waters of the St. Lawrence system, and almost the entire continent was claimed by the French as belonging to New France. As far as appears, there were no Indians having settled abodes on the north shore of Lake Erie for more than a century after the expulsion of the Neutrals. Nor does any attempt appear to have been made by the whites to explore south-western Ontario until the close of the last century. The Iroquois continued for a long period to range its forests for beaver in the winter. The rivalry between the French and the English for the control of the vast western fur trade led to the erection of outposts by the English at Oswego and by the French at Cataraqui, Niagara, Detroit and Michilimakinac, during the latter part of the 17th century. English traders sailed or paddled up the lakes to get their share of the traffic, and were from time to time summarily arrested and expelled by their rivals. Both parties tried to ingratiate themselves with the natives. The French were as eager to maintain a state of warfare between the Iroquois and the Indians of the upper lakes —the Hurons, Ottawas, Pottawatamies, Ojibways etc.—as to induce the former to keep the peace with the white inhabitants of Canada. There were two great trade routes to Montreal, viz: by Mackinac, the Georgian Bay and the French and Ottawa River and by Detroit, Lake Erie and Niagara ; the Lake Simcoe portage routes by the Trent River system, and the Holland River and Toronto were also used. Trading or military parties, under the leadership of La Salle, Tonty, Perrot, Du Lhut, Cadaillac, passed along the coast of L. Erie in canoes; but little record if any remained of their visits to the shores. Kettle Creek was long called the Tonty River. It is so named in one of Bellin's maps of 1755, and by the Canadian Land Board at Detroit as lately as 1793. The only northern tributaries of Lake Erie to which names are given on the map of 1755 are the Grand River, River D'Ollier (Patterson's Creek), which in some maps is called the River of the Wintering—a manifest reference to Galinee and Dollier de Casson's sojourn in 1669–70—the River a la Barbue (Catfish Creek), the River Tonty (Kettle Creek) a little east of P'te au Fort (Plum Point or else Port Talbot) and the River aux Cedres (M'Gregor's Creek in Essex). The Thames is described as a "River unknown to all geographers, and which "you go up eighty leagues without finding any rapids (*saults*)." The Chenail Ecarte is indicated as the only outlet of the Sydenham river the map-makers assuming that Walpole Island was part of the mainland. The mouths of four or five streams are shown between Long Point and "the Little Lake" (Rondeau), and the shore is marked "The High Cliffs." "The Low Cliffs" were between the Rondeau and Point Pelee. In one of Bellin's maps of 1755 in the present writer's possession Long Point is shown as a peninsula, and the streams now in the County of Elgin are marked "Unknown Rivers," but the map firstly mentioned and published in the same year, is more complete, represents Long Point as an island, and names the Barbue and Touty rivers and Fort Point, (*P'te au Fort*) which are not named in the other. The Tonty, moreover, is represented as an inlet by way of distinction from the other streams (including the Barbue) which appear as of equal insignificance. The naming of Kettle Creek after the great explorer and devoted lieutenant of La Salle indicates its consequence. Its harbor was of paramount importance to the navigation of these early days, but no doubt the portage route extending from its mouth to the Thames exalted the little river in the eyes of the explorers who honored it with Tonty's name. (*i*).

THE INDIAN TITLE.

On July 19th, 1701, the Iroquois ceded to the British the entire country between the lakes, "including the country where "beavers and all sorts of wild game keep, and the place called " De Tret," (*j*) but this appears to have been a mere formality as no possession was taken by the purchasers.

The Ojibways have a tradition that they defeated the Iroquois (called by them the Nottawas or Nahdoways) in a succession of skirmishes, ending in a complete victory at the outlet of Burlington Bay, and the final expulsion of the Six Nations from that part of Ontario between the Great Lakes. The Ojibways then spread east and west over the country. "A "treaty of peace and friendship was then made with the " Nahdoways residing on the south side of Lake Ontario, and "both nations solemnly covenanted, by going through the usual "forms of burying the tomahawk, smoking the pipe of peace, "and locking their hands and arms together, agreeing in future "to call each other *Brothers*. Thus ended their war with the " Nahdoways," (*k*)

(*i*) General John S. Clarke, of Auburn, N. Y., in correspondence with the present writer, dwells upon the importance of the Kettle Creek portage route in the seventeenth century. He is a recognized authority upon the subject of Indian trade routes.
(*j*) History of Middlesex County, p. 17.
(*k*) "Peter Jones and the Ojebway Indians," p. 113.

Whatever may be the truth of the details, there is no doubt of the fact that the Ojibways or their kindred the Mississagas were the sole occupants of Western Ontario at the time of the conquest in 1759, except near the Detroit River where the remnant of the Hurons or Wyandots had settled. It was with the Mississagas that the British negotiated in 1784 for the cession of the country from the " head of the Lake Ontario or the Creek " Waghguata to the River La Tranche, then down the river "until a south course will strike the mouth of Cat Fish Creek " on Lake Erie." On the 21st May, 1790, Alexander M'Kee announced to the Land-board at Detroit the cession to the Crown by the Indians of that part of Upper Canada west of the former grant. The surrender of the Indian title opened the way in each division of the lake shore district for settlement. *

CHARLEVOIX'S DESCRIPTION.

In the year 1721 the distinguished traveller, Charlevoix, passed through Lake Erie on his way up the Lakes and thence down the Mississippi to New Orleans. The north shore of Lake Erie, and chiefly that part now embraced within the limits of the County of Elgin, is singled out by him as the most beautiful country he met with in his passage. Many travellers since Charlevoix have admired the charming scenery at the mouths of Otter, Catfish, Kettle and Talbot Creeks, but few if any have described it so well. As Colonel Talbot was influenced mainly by Charlevoix's description of the country to establish his settlement at the outlet of Talbot Creek in 1803, the present writer makes no apology for reproducing the following extended passage from the celebrated and gifted traveller:

NOTE.—The explanatory notes referring to the extract are by the late Leonidas Burwell, M. P. P., and are given by him in a letter to His Honor, Judge Hughes, which has been kindly presented by the recipient to the Elgin Historical and Scientific Institute.

* The north shore of Lake Erie appears to have been so little known to the officials, that Kettle Creek and Cat Fish Creek were continually confused and taken as being one or different streams as chance would have it. The Land-board considered that a surrender of the lands west of Kettle Creek gave the Crown all the territory not previously ceded. The Indians at Detroit who made the cession were the Ojibways, Hurons, Ottawas and Pottawatamies.

"The 28th May, 1721, I went eighteen leagues and found
"myself over against the *great river* which comes from the
"East in forty-two degrees fifteen minutes. Nevertheless the
"great trees were not yet green. This country appeared to me
"to be very fine. We made very little way the 29th and none
"at all the 30th. We embarked the next day about sun rise,
"and went forward apace. The first of June being Whitsunday,
"after going up a pretty river almost an hour which comes a
"great way, and runs between two fine meadows, we made a
"portage about sixty paces to escape going round a point which
"advances fifteen leagues into the lake: they call it the *Long
"Point*. It is very sandy and produces naturally many vines. (*l*)

"The following days I saw nothing remarkable, but I coasted
"a charming country that was hid from time to time by some dis-
"agreeable skreens, but of little depth. In every place where I
"landed I was enchanted with the beauty and variety of land-
"scape bounded by the finest forest in the world; besides this
"water fowl swarmed everywhere. I cannot say there is such
"plenty of game in the woods: but I know that on the south side
"there are vast herds of wild cattle. (*m*)

"If one always travelled as I did then, with a clear sky
"and charming climate on water as bright as the finest
"fountain, and were to meet everywhere with safe and pleasant
"encampings, where one might find all manner of game at little
"cost, breathing at one's ease a pure air, and enjoying the sight
"of the finest countries, one would be tempted to travel all one's
"life."

"It put me in mind of those ancient patriarchs who had no
"fixed abode, dwelt under tents, were in some manner master
' of all the countries they travelled over, and peaceably enjoyed
"all their productions without having the trouble which is
"inavoidable in the possession of a real domain. How many

(*l*) This river is what is now known as "Big Creek" and answers this description at the present day. It enters the lake a little above Port Rowan.

(*m*) This charming country is evidently, the greater part of it, the County of Elgin, as the portage is not more than thirteen miles from the boundary line of Bayham. In passing up the lake one would meet with a great variety of landscape as the sand-hills in Houghton and the mouths of the Otter, Catfish and other creeks would be passed. The lofty pines and chestnuts and oaks along this coast, in their original state no doubt appeared like the "finest forest in the world."

"oaks represented to me that of *Mamre?* How many fountains "made me remember that of Jacob? Every day a situation of "my own choosing, a neat and convenient house set up and "furnished with necessaries in a quarter of an hour, spread with "flowers always fresh, on a fine green carpet, and on every side "plain and natural beauties which art had not altered and "which it can not imitate. If the pleasures suffer some inter- "ruption either by bad weather or some unforseen accident, they "are the more relished when they reappear.

"If I had a mind to moralize, I should add, these alterna- "tions of pleasure and disappointment which I have so often "experienced since I have been travelling, are very proper to "make us sensible that there is no kind of life more capable of "representing to us continually that we are only on the earth "like pilgrims, and that we can only use, as in passing, the goods "of this world ; that a man wants but a few things; and that "we ought to take with patience the misfortunes that happen "in our journey, since they pass away equally, and with the "same celerity. In short how many things in travelling make "us sensible of the dependence in which we live upon Divine "providence, which does not make use of, for this mixture of "good and evil, men's passions, but the vicissitudes of the seasons "which we may foresee, and of the caprice of the elements, "which we may expect of course. Of consequence, how easy is "it, and how many opportunities have we to merit by our "dependence on and resignation to the will of God ?

"They say commonly that long voyages do not make people "religious, but nothing one would think should be more capable "of making them so, than the scenes they go through."

THE BRITISH OCCUPATION.

The conquest of Canada in 1759 was followed by the occupation of Detroit and the upper forts by a British force under the famous Major Robert Rogers. He followed the south shore of Lake Erie, and near the site of Cleveland was met by the celebrated Ottawa chief, Pontiac, who challenged his right to pass through the country without the formal permission of its savage sovereign. The operations of the conspiracy of Pontiac (1763-5) are described in Parkman's glowing pages. The success of the American Revolution was followed by the settlement not only of the U. E. Loyalists but also of many of the disbanded British troops in the most fertile districts north of the lakes. To locate these advantageously a Land-board was established at Detroit by the Canadian Government and it continued to perform its functions until the surrender of that post to the United States under the provisions of the Jay Treaty of 1794.

McNIFF'S EXPLORATION.

The Indian title to the whole north shore region having been surrendered to the Crown, no time was lost in opening the territory for settlement. Patrick McNiff, an assistant surveyor attached to the Ordinance Department, was ordered by Patrick Murray, Commandant at Detroit, to explore the north shore from Long Point westward and investigate the quality and situation of the land. His report is dated 16th June 1790. The following extract is interesting:

"From Pointe aux Pins to the portage at Long Point, no
"possibility of making any settlement to front on the Lake,
"being all the way a yellow and white sand bank from 50 to 100
"feet high, top covered with chestnut and scrubby oak and no
"harbours where even light boats may enter except River Tonty
"and River a la Barbue. (n) A load boat may enter the latter
"having four and a half feet water on the bar; on each side of
"River a la Barbue are flats of excellent lands, but not above
"fifteen or twenty chains wide, before very high land commences,
"which in many places does not appear to be accessible for any
"carriage. On the tops of these very high hills, good land,
"timber, some very large chestnut, hickory and bass. These
"hills are separated by dry ravines almost impassable from their
"great depth—on the back of Long Point very good land, not so
"hilly as what I have passed. Timber bass, black walnut and

(n) Kettle and Catfish Creeks.

"hard maple, but marshy in front for twenty or thirty chains. (o)

In consequence of this unfavorable report, townships were directed to be laid out on the River Thames, instead of the lake shore.

LIEUTENANT-GOVERNOR SIMCOE.

In the year 1791 the Quebec Act was passed, dividing Quebec into two provinces, and Colonel John Graves Simcoe became the first lieutenant-governor of Upper Canada. Before the Bill was introduced into parliament, it was understood that Simcoe had been selected by Pitt to govern the new province, direct its settlement and establish constitutional government after the model of the British system. As early as January, 1791, he had written a letter to Sir Joseph Banks, President of the Royal Society, (p) in which after mentioning his appointment, he explained his own plans as to the administration, and stated his desire to profit by the ideas of his correspondent whom he would wait upon for that purpose.

" For the purpose of commerce, union and power, I propose
" that the site of the colony should be in that Great Peninsula
" between the Lakes Huron, Erie and Ontario, a spot destined by
" nature, sooner or later, to govern the interior world.

"I mean to establish a capital in the very heart of the
" country, upon the River La Tranche, which is navigable for
" batteauxs for 150 miles—and near to where the Grand River,
" which falls into Erie, and others that communicate with Huron
" and Ontario almost interlock. The capital I mean to call
" Georgina—and aim to settle in its vicinity Loyalists, who are
" now in Connecticut, provided that the Government approve of
" the system."

As a member of the House of Commons, Simcoe spoke in support of a provision in the bill for the establishment of an hereditary nobility, which Fox had moved to strike out. The report states that Colonel Simcoe " having pronounced a pane-

---

(o) Record book of the Land Board at Detroit, now in the Crown Lands Department at Toronto.

"gyric on the British constitution, wished it to be adopted in the "present instance, as far as circumstances would admit." The provision was in the bill as finally passed.

Having proceeded to Quebec to enter upon the performance of his duties, he appears to have utilized every opportunity for informing himself of his new domain. He writes to Hon. Henry Dundas from Montreal, December 7, 1791, in a letter marked "secret and confidential," as follows:—

"I am happy to have found in the surveyor's office an actual "survey of the River La Tranche. It answers my most "sanguine expectations, and I have but little doubt that its "communications with the Ontario and Erie will be found to be "very practicable, the whole forming a route which, in all "respects, may annihilate the political consequences of Niagara "and Lake Erie. * * * * My ideas at present are to "assemble the new corps, artificers, etc., at Cataraqui (Kingston), "and to take its present garrison and visit Toronto and the "heads of La Tranche, to pass down that river to Detroit, and "early in the spring to occupy such a central position as shall be "previously chosen for the capital."

On the 16th July, 1792, the name of the River La Tranche was changed to the Thames by proclamation of the Governor, issued at Kingston. In the spring, he had written that "Toronto "appears to be the natural arsenal of Lake Ontario and to afford "an easy access overland to Lake Huron." He adds: "The "River La Tranche, near the navigable head of which I propose "to establish the Capital, by what I can gather from the few "people who have visited it, will afford a safe, more certain, and "I am inclined to think, by taking due advantage of the season, "a less expensive route to Detroit than that of Niagara."

At Quebec Simcoe had met the Hon. Thomas Talbot, who had joined the 24th Regiment as Lieutenant in the previous year. Talbot was then a young man of twenty, whilst Simcoe was in his fortieth year. A strong attachment sprang up between these two remarkable men, and Talbot accompanied the lieutenant-governor to Niagara, in the capacity of private and confidential secretary. After meeting the first Legislature elected in Upper Canada during the fall of 1792 Simcoe decided to make a journey overland to Detroit. He left Navy Hall on the 4th February, 1793, and returned on the 10th March. His travelling companions were Capt. Fitzgerald, Lieutenant Smith (previously Secretary to the Detroit Land Board, subsequently the first Surveyor General of Upper Canada, an M. P. P.,Speaker of the House, etc, and afterward created a baronet), Lieutenants Talbot, Gray, Givens and Major Littlehales. All of these were prominent afterward in the history of the Province. Talbot became the founder of the Talbot Settlement. Gray was appointed Solicitor General ; he perished in the schooner 'Speedy' on Lake Ontario in 1804 with Judge Cochrane, Sheriff Macdonell and others. Givens was afterward the well-known Colonel Givens, Superintendant of Indian Affairs at York. Littlehales was afterward Sir E. B. Littlehales, Secretary of War for Ireland, during the Lord-Lieutenancy of the Marquis of Cornwallis; he married in 1805 the Lady Elizabeth Fitzgerald, daughter of the Duke of Leinster and sister of the unfortunate Lord Edward Fitzgerald. (*p*)

The journey was made partly in sleighs but chiefly on foot. Littlehales kept a diary of the occurrences on the way. The route was by Ten-mile Creek, Nelles' house at the Grand River, the Mohawk Indian village (a little below Brantford), the portage route to the Forks of the Thames (London), and then down or along the River to Detroit. Joseph Brant with about a dozen of his Indians accompanied the party from the Mohawk Village to Delaware, doubtless to furnish them with game and guide them over the long portage. The Indians excited admiration by their skill in constructing wigwams of elm bark to lodge the company. After leaving the Grand River the trail passed a Mississaga encampment, a trader's house, fine open deer plains, several beaver dams, "an encampment said to have been "Lord Fitzgerald's when on his march to Detroit, Michilimacki- "nac and the Mississippi," a cedar grove ; crossed a small branch of the La Tranche, and the main branch soon afterwards; "went between an irregular fence of stakes made by the "Indians to intimidate and impede the deer, and facilitate their "hunting;" again they crossed the main branch of the Thames,(*q*)

(*p*) Dr. Scadding's notes to his reprint of Littlehales' Journal.

(*q*) This was no doubt where London now is.

and "halted to observe a beautiful situation, formed by a bend
"of the river—a grove of hemlock and pine, and a large creek.
"We passed some deep ravines and made our wigwam by a
"stream on the brow of a hill, near a spot where Indians were
"interred. The burying ground was of earth raised, nearly
"covered with leaves; and wickered over—adjoining it was a
"large pole, with painted hieroglyphics on it denoting the
"nation, tribes and achievements of the deceased, either as
"chiefs, warriors, or hunters." This was on the 13th February.
The food of the party consisted of soup and dried venison, to
which squirrel and racoon meat added variety. Littlehales
remarks about the latter: "The three racoons when roasted
"made us an excellent supper. Some parts were rancid,
"but in general the flesh was exceedingly tender and good." On
the 14th they encamped a few miles above the Delaware village.
During the day the diarist had "observed many trees blazed,
"and various figures of Indians (returning from battle with
"scalps) and animals drawn upon them, descriptive of the
"nations, tribes and number that had passed. Many of them
"were well drawn, especially a bison."

"This day we walked over very uneven ground, and passed
"two lakes of about four miles in circumference, between which
"were many fine larch trees."

Next morning they walked on the ice of the river five or
six miles to the Delaware village, where the chiefs received them
cordially and regaled them with eggs and venison "Captain
"Brant being obliged to return to a council of the Six Nations,
"we stayed the whole day. The Delaware Castle is pleasantly
"situated upon the banks of the Thames; the meadows at the
"bottom are cleared to some extent, and in summer planted with
"Indian corn. After walking twelve or fourteen miles this day,
"part of the way through plains of white oak and ash, and
"passing several Chippawa Indians upon their hunting parties,
"and in their encampments, we arrived at a Canadian trader's;
"and a little beyond, in proceeding down the river the Indians
"discovered a spring of an oily nature, which upon examination
"proved to be a kind of petroleum. We passed another wigwam
"of Chippawas, making maple sugar, the mildness of the winter
"having compelled them in a great measure to abandon their

"annual hunting. We soon arrived at an old hut where we "passed the night."

On the 17th, after a journey of four or five miles, they passed the Moravian Village which had been begun in May, 1792. The Delaware Indians were "under the control, and in many particu- "lars, under the command of four missionaries, Messrs. Zeis- "berger, Senseman, Edwards and Young." They were making progress towards civilization, and already had corn fields and were being instructed in different branches of agriculture. " At "this place every respect was paid to the Governor, and we "procured a seasonable refreshment of eggs, milk and butter. "Pursuing our journey eight or nine miles, we stopped for the "night at the extremity of a new road, cut by the Indians and "close to a creek."

"18th—Crossing the Thames and leaving behind us a new log "house, belonging to a sailor named Carpenter, we passed a "thick, swampy wood of black walnut, where His Excellency's "servant was lost for three or four hours. We then came to a "bend of the La Tranche (Thames) (r) and were agreeably "surprised to meet twelve or fourteen carioles coming to meet "and conduct the Governor, who, with his suite, got into them, "and at about four o'clock arrived at Dolsen's, having previously "reconnoitred a fork of the river, and examined a mill of "curious construction erecting upon it. The settlement where "Dolsen resides is very promising, the land is well adapted for "farmers, and there are some respectable inhabitants on both "sides of the river; behind it to the south is a range of spacious "meadows—elk are continually seen upon them—and the pools "and ponds are full of cray fish."

"From Dolsen's we went to the mouth of the Thames in "carioles, about twelve miles, and saw the remains of a consider- "able town of the Chippawas, where, it is reported, a desperate "battle was fought between them and the Senecas, and upon "which occasion the latter, being totally vanquished, abandoned "their dominions to the conquerors. Certain it is, that human "bones are scattered in abundance in the vicinity of the ground, "and the Indians have a variety of traditions relative to this

---

(r) Afterwards referred to by the diarist as the high bank.

"transaction." *

We pass over briefly the Governor's reception at Detroit. The Canadian militia on the east bank fired a *feu de joie*. He crossed the river in boats amidst floating ice. The garrison of Detroit was under arms to receive His Majesty's representative. A royal salute was fired.

The farms, the apple orchards, windmills and houses close together on the river bank gave an appearance of population and respectability. Talbot's regiment, the 24th, was stationed at Detroit. Fort Lenoult and the rest of the works were inspected. The party visited at the River Rouge a sloop almost ready to be launched. They went to see the Bloody Bridge, memorable for the slaughter of British troops by Pontiac 30 years before.

On the 23rd, the Governor left Detroit on his homeward journey, Col. McKee, Mr. Baby and others escorting His Excellency as far as the high bank where the carioles had met the party on the 18th. " Here we separated; and each taking his "pack or knapsack on his back, we walked that night to the " Moravian village."

On the 27th the chiefs at the village entertained the party with venison, and dancing, "a ceremony they never dispense " with when any of the King's officers of rank visit their " villages."

"28th.—At six we stopped at an old Mississaga hut, upon the " south side of the Thames. After taking some refreshment of " salt pork and venison, well cooked by Lieutenant Smith, who " superintended that department, we, as usual, sang God Save " the King, and went to rest."

"March 1st.—We set out along the banks of the river; " then, ascending a high hill, quitted our former path, and " directed our course to the northward. A good deal of snow " having fallen, and lying still on the ground, we saw tracks of " otters, deer, wolves and bears and other animals many of which " being quite fresh induced the Mohawks to pursue them, but " without success. We walked 14 or 15 miles and twice crossed " the river, and a few creeks, upon the ice ; once we came close

---

* Note Peter Jones' statement as quoted on page 28.

"to a Chippawa hunting camp, opposite to a fine terrace, on the
"banks of which we encamped, near a bay. * * * 2nd.—
"We struck the Thames at one end of a low flat island
"enveloped with shrubs and trees; the rapidity and strength of
"the current were such as to have forced a channel through
"the main land, being a peninsula, and to have formed the
"island. We walked over a rich meadow, and at its extremity
"came to the forks of the river. (s) The Governor wished to
"examine this situation and its environs; and we therefore
"remained here all the day. He judged it to be a situation
"eminently calculated for the metropolis of Canada.. Among
"many other essentials, it possesses the following advantages:
"command of territory,—internal situation,—central position,—
"facility of water communication up and down the Thames
"into Lakes St. Clair, Erie, Huron and Superior,—navigable
"for boats to near its source, and for small crafts probably to
"the Moravian settlement—to the northward by a small portage
"to the waters flowing into Lake Huron—to the south-east by
"a carrying place into Lake Ontario and the River St. Lawrence;
"the soil luxuriantly fertile,—the land rich, and capable of being
"easily cleared, and soon put into a state of agriculture,—a
"pinery upon an adjacent high knoll, and other timber on the
"heights, well calculated for the erection of public buildings,—a
"climate not inferior to any part of Canada."

"To these natural advantages an object of great consideration
"is to be added, that the enormous expenses of the Indian
"Department would be greatly diminished, if not abolished
"the Indians would, in all probability, be induced to become the
"carriers of their own peltries, and they would find a ready,
"contiguous, commodious, and equitable mart, honorably ad-
"vantageous to Government, and the community in general,
"without their becoming a prey to the monopolizing and
"unprincipled trader."

"The young Indians, who had chased a herd of deer in
"company with Lieutenant Givens, returned unsuccessful, but
"brought with them a large porcupine; which was very
"seasonable, as our provisions were nearly expended. This

(s) Now the city of London.

" animal afforded us a very good repast, and tasted like a pig.
" The Newfoundland dog attempted to bite the porcupine, but
" soon got his mouth filled with the barbed quills, which gave
" him exquisite pain. An Indian undertook to extract them,
" and with much perseverance plucked them out, one by one, and
" carefully applied a root or decoction, which speedily healed the
" wound."

" Various figures were delineated on trees at the forks of the
" River Thames, done with charcoal and vermillion; the most
" remarkable were the imitations of men with deer's heads"

" We saw a fine eagle on the wing, and two or three large
" birds, perhaps vultures."

" 3rd.—We were glad to leave our wigwam early this
" morning, it having rained incessantly the whole night; besides,
" the hemlock branches on which we slept were wet before they
" were gathered for our use.—We first ascended the height at
" least 120 feet into a continuation of the pinery already
" mentioned; quitting that, we came to a beautiful plain with
" detached clumps of white oak, and open woods; then crossing
" a creek running into the south branch of the Thames, we
" entered a thick swampy wood, where we were at a loss to
" discover any track; but in a few minutes we were released
" from this dilemma by the Indians, who making a cast, soon
" descried our old path to Detroit. Descending a hill and
" crossing a brook, we came at noon to the encampment we left
" on the 14th of February, and were agreeably surprised by
" meeting Captain Brant and a numerous retinue; among them
" were four of the Indians we had despatched to him when we
" first altered our course for the forks of the River Thames."

On the 4th, after crossing brooks and rivulets, much swollen by a thunder-storm, and passing the hut occupied by them on the 12th February they noticed " very fine beech trees."

Next day:—"We again crossed one of the branches of the
" south-east fork of the Thames, and halted in a cypress or cedar
" grove, where we were much amused by seeing Brant and the
" Indians chase a lynx with their dogs and rifle guns, but they
" did not catch it. Several porcupines were seen."

On the 6th they reached the Mohawk village, crossing the river at a different place and by a nearer route than before. The

Indians had met the Governor with horses at "the end of the "plain, near the Salt Lick Creek." The party finally arrived at Navy Hall on the 10th day of March.

At this period the overland route from Detroit to Niagara was apparently well known. There was an annual "Winter-"express" each way, which Simcoe met on his westward journey on the 12th February and on his homeward route on the 5th March. Littlehales mentions a Mr. Clarke as being with it on each occasion. On their first meeting, the express was accompanied by a Wyandot and a Chippawa Indian. The second time, Mr. Augustus Jones, the surveyor, was either with or following it. He surveyed the north-west part of Southwold in the following year. On the up trip, the Governor's party met one man, who afterward proved to be a runaway thief from Detroit. They were also overtaken by a traveller, who, as they were subsequently informed, had got himself supplied with provisions and horses to the Grand River, and a guide from thence to Detroit, by the false representation that he had despatches for the Governor. "He quitted us under the "plausible pretence of looking for land to establish a settlement."

It appears that immediately after the capture of Niagara by Johnston in 1759, merchants from New England and Virginia had rushed in to participate in the fur-trade, which until that time had been largely monopolized by the French. As might be expected, many lawless acts were committed by these adventurers, and various proceedings were adopted by the Government to check and control them. After the American Revolution land-hunters came into the peninsula and undertook to purchase lands directly from the Indians. These purchases were ignored by the Land Boards, who always repudiated the idea that the Indians were proprietors of the land. No steps were taken however to locate settlers until the Indian title by occupancy was surrendered to the Crown. Even then, Simcoe's first step was to procure surveys for the purpose of establishing military roads, fortified posts, dockyards, etc., in order that when the settlers came they might be easily defended against hostile attacks, whether from the Indians, the United States troops, or the French or Spanish, who it was believed might invade the province by way of the Mississippi, the Ohio and the upper lakes.

Patrick McNiff's survey of the River Thames, as far as the upper Delaware village, was finished in 1793. His map is dated at Detroit on the 25th June of this year. In it he mentions that "from the entrance to the 12th lot of the 3rd township was "surveyed two years since, from the 12th lot * * to the "upper village was surveyed in April and May 1793."

The map gives the "road leading from the Delawares to the "Moravian village," "corn-fields" along the east bank of the river, an Indian village in the Southwold bend, and opposite on the southerly bank the "road leading to the entrance of Kettle "Creek (*t*) on Lake Erie. Five hours' journey." It also shows the road leading to the Mohawk village on the Grand River.

The Moravian village is near the site of the battle field, and it is marked "commenced in May, 1792." The present location of Dundas Street and the Longwoods Road would appear to correspond with the roads east and west of Delaware as laid down. (*u*) Simcoe in forwarding McNiff's survey to Mr. Dundas on 20th September, 1793, thus refers to the Lake Erie region :

"The tract of country which lies between the river (or rather "navigable canal as its Indian name and French translation "import) and Lake Erie, is one of the finest for all agricultural "purposes in North America, and far exceeds the soil or climate "of the Atlantic States. There are few or no interjacent "swamps, and a variety of useful streams empty themselves into "the lake or the river."

The Governor makes frequent reference in his correspondence and state papers to his plans for establishing the capital, of Upper Canada at the upper forks of the Thames, to be called Georgina, London or New London. Down to the very time of his departure in 1796, and after the seat of government had been transferred to York (now Toronto), he regarded the latter as but a temporary capital, the real metropolis having yet to be built at London in accordance with his original design.

Talbot remained in the service of the Lieutenant Governor

(*t*) This disposes of the story told by Colonel Talbot to Mrs. Jamieson in 1837. He informed her that the name originated from his men having lost a kettle in the creek. But the creek was called Riviere a la Chaudiere or Kettle River by the French, and that is one of the names given to it in D. W. Smith's Gazetteer, of Upper Canada published in 1799.

(*u*) The writer has not been able to see Mr. McNiff's report upon this survey.

until June 1794, when as Major of the 5th Regiment he departed for England under orders for Flanders, carrying with him special letters of recommendation from Simcoe to Dundas and to Mr. King, the Under Secretary of State. He had been employed in various confidential missions. In 1793 he had been sent to Philadelphia to await news from Europe, when war with France was believed to be imminent. On the 22nd August, 1793, we find Talbot in "the most confidential inter-"course with the several Indian tribes," as Simcoe expresses it, at the Miamis Rapids, where he had met the United States Commissioners and the Confederated Indians to consider the boundary question. In April, 1794, Simcoe was himself at the Falls of the Miami, and he repeated the visit during the following September, going by way of Fort Erie. This visit was a prolonged one; for we find that in October he met an Indian Council at Brown's Town in the Miami country. It is probable Talbot accompanied him in his capacity as military secretary. The construction by Simcoe of the fort at the foot of the rapids of the Miami in the spring of that year was an audacious step, which might easily have produced a new war between the United States and England, although Simcoe believed it had had the opposite result, and prevented war. All disputes between the two nations were however concluded by the treaty of 1794, usually called the Jay Treaty. Provision was made for the abandonment of the frontier posts hitherto occupied by English garrisons. Forts Niagara, Detroit, Miami and Michilimackinac received American garrisons in 1796 or shortly thereafter; English troops were stationed in new forts at St. Joseph's Island, Malden, Turkey Point, Fort Erie, Toronto, etc. The English flag floated no longer south of the great lakes. During the year 1796, Simcoe went to England on leave of absence, and he never returned to Canada.

COLONEL TALBOT.

The Honorable Thomas Talbot received his company and his majority in the same year, 1793. He was Colonel of the Fifth Regiment in 1795, at the early age of twenty-five. After eight years of military service on the Continent, partly in Flanders and partly at Gibraltar, he was still in 1803 a young man with every prospect that is usually considered alluring to ambition. Suddenly, to the amazement of his friends and the public, he abandoned the brilliant career upon which he had entered under so favorable auspices, cut himself loose from civilization itself, and buried himself in the recesses of the Canadian forest. He determined to settle on the north shore of Lake Erie, where he had previously selected a location on one of his journeyings with Governor Simcoe. Talbot had formed plans for diverting the stream of immigration from the United States, or rather for continuing its current as far as Upper Canada. He would attract settlers from New York, Pennsylvania and New England, who were dissatisfied with republican institutions or allured by the fertility of the Lake Erie region, and would build up a loyal British community, under the laws and institutions of the mother land.

It was a memorable event in the history of the County of Elgin, when on the 21st day of May, 1803, landing at Port Talbot, he took an axe and chopped down the first tree, thus inaugurating what has since been known as the Talbot Settlement. Henceforward, Colonel Talbot, Port Talbot, the Talbot Road, and the Talbot Settlement, are names inseparably connected with the history of the making of Upper Canada.

At that time the nearest settlement on Lake Erie was near Turkey Point, 60 miles away. In 1802 there was but one settled minister west of Niagara, Father Marchand, of Sandwich, a Roman Catholic priest. There were but seven clergymen settled in the whole Province. The record (v) states, however, that " Besides, there are several missionaries of the Methodistical " order, whose residence is not fixed." Even at that early day the circuit-rider threaded the maze of forest between the Long Point clearings and those near the mouth of the Thames, and made his way down the Detroit River to.the Essex shore of Lake Erie, where there was a fringe of settlement. But, generally speaking, the country north of Lake Erie to the borders of Lake Huron and the Georgian Bay was still a wilderness of continuous unbroken forest.

(v) Tiffany's Upper Canada Almanac, Niagara, 1802.

TORONTO.

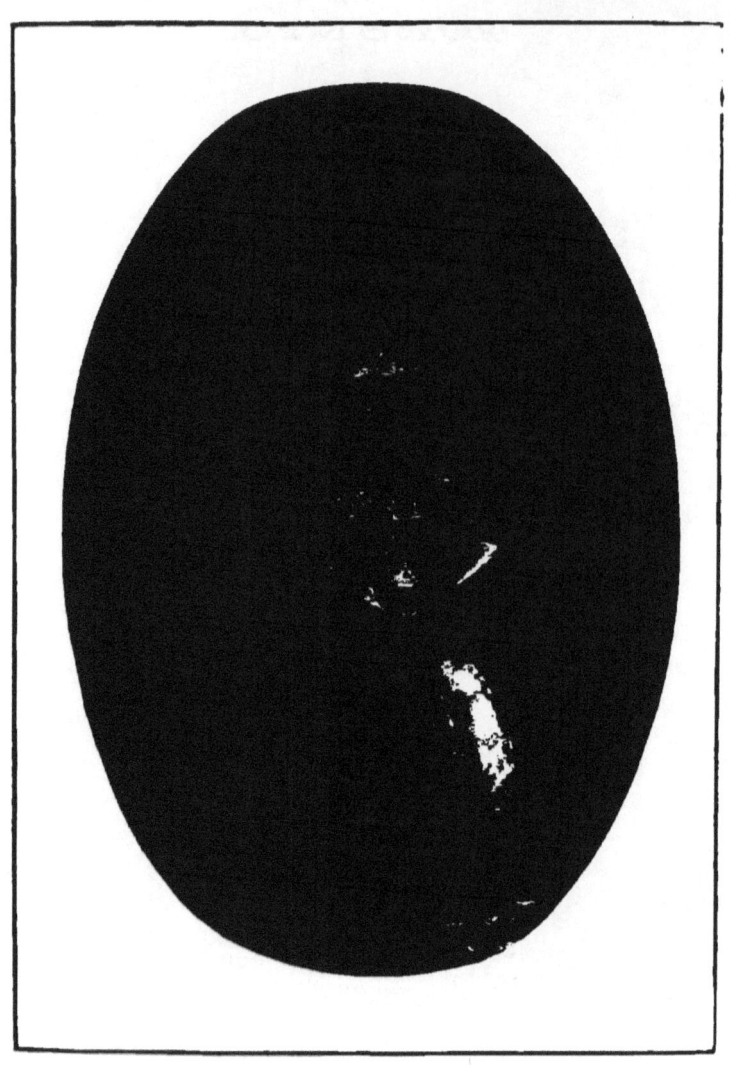

COLONEL TALBOT.

THE TALBOT SETTLEMENT.

—BY—

C. O. ERMATINGER.

THE TALBOT SETTLEMENT—with which civilized life in this and surrounding counties began–may be said to have commenced with the nineteenth century. Colonel Talbot, the founder of the Settlement, is said to have traversed the tract now comprising the County of Elgin in company with Lieutenant-Governor Simcoe, proceeding from the lake shore to the forks of the Thames, before the dawn of the century. (*a*)

Whether this may be accepted as an historical fact or not, it is manifest the Colonel must, before forming his plan of settlement, have been possessed of some information regarding the Township of Yarmouth and country surrounding it, leading him to believe it suitable for the purpose he formed, "as being from the nature of the soil favorable to his design of raising hemp for exportation, and also affording scope for the establishment of such a number of families as may be induced to follow him into the province." (*b*) It may be said that his subsequent abandonment of the hemp industry indicates that he had no personal knowledge of the locality before he settled in it. Yet, the fact remains that he did select this locality for some reason and did settle it.

The Honorable Thomas Talbot was born at Malahide, County of Dublin, Ireland, 17th July, 1771. His parents Richard Talbot and Margaret Baroness Talbot, were of the Talbots of Malahide Castle, a family descended from Richard de Talbot, of the time of William the Conqueror and ancestor of the Earl of Shrewsbury. "Apart from its achievements, this is one of the oldest families in the English aristocracy which traces alike its

---

(a) E. Ermatinger's Life of Col. Talbot, Page 13.
(b) See extract from Lord Hobart's letter dated 15th February, 1803, app. to Journal of Assembly U. C., 1836, No. 22.

descent and its surname from the Norman conquerors of England; and it may really be said that there has hardly been a time during the last eight hundred years in which the Talbots have not been of considerable account in public life." (*bb*)

Colonel Talbot's early education was obtained in the public free school of Manchester, and at the age of eleven years he obtained a commission in the army, and became at the age of 17 or 18 years one of the *aides-de-camp* to a relative, then Lord Lieutenant of Ireland, the Marquis of Buckingham. Arthur Wellesley, afterwards the renowned "Iron Duke" of Wellington, was his brother *aide*. This was in 1786-88. These two companions in early years renewed their acquaintance at long intervals. They met for the last time at the advanced age of four-score years and doubtless indulged in a retrospect of their so widely divided lives. The great Duke died 14th September 1852; Colonel Talbot on 6th February 1853. The Duke of Wellington had accomplished a life work of the greatest consequence to the whole of Europe. Colonel Talbot's life work, though carried on in comparative obscurity, was of equal consequence to the settlers of the Talbot settlement, in far off Canada, and their descendants.

In 1790, Mr. Talbot joined the 24th Regiment, as Lieutenant at Quebec, and in the following year was attached to the suite of the first Lieutenant-Governor of Upper Canada, General Simcoe, with whom he continued as his private and confidential secretary some four years, when he joined his regiment in Europe, having previously received both his company and majority. In January 1796 he became Lieutenant-Colonel of the 5th Regiment of Foot, with which he served on the continent, and at Gibralter, until the Peace of Amiens.

Early in the year 1803 Colonel Talbot applied to the Home Government for a grant of land in the "distant Township of Yarmouth in the County of Norfolk." (*c*) His application was

---

(*bb*) Encyclopedia Brittanica 9th ed. vol. 23, p. 25.

(*c*) See extract from Lord Hobart's letter already referred to. Also letter of General Simcoe, dated 11th February, 1803. It is elsewhere pointed out in this volume that Yarmouth was then in the County of Suffolk as constituted by the U. C. Legislature, though immediately adjoining the County of Norfolk on the West.

endorsed by General Simcoe in a letter in which he speaks of Colonel Talbot and of his services to himself and the colony in terms of the highest praise, and especially in the confidential measures he took for the preservation of peace, for "his most confidential intercourse with the several Indian Tribes, and occasionally with His Majesty's Minister at Philadelphia," — which duties without any salary or emolument, he executed to the Lieutenant-Governor's "perfect satisfaction."

"I consider these circumstances," continues General Simcoe addressing Lord Hobart, "as authorizing me in general terms to recommend Mr. Talbot to your consideration and protection. Mr. Talbot's specific application, which I beg leave to support to the utmost of my power, consists of two points. The first is the grant of five thousand acres of land as a field officer, actually and *bona-fide* meaning to reside in the Province for the purpose of establishing himself therein. The king's bounty having been extended to the field officers who had served during the American war, in grants to a similar extent (exclusive of an allotment for every individual which their families might consist of) it was judged expedient by myself, Mr. Chief Justice Osgoode, and other confidential officers of the Crown in that colony, to extend the provision of five thousand acres to any field officer of character, who, *bona-fide*, should become a settler therein, it being obvous that it was for His Majesty's interest that a loyal set of European gentlemen should, as speedily as possible, be obtained to take the lead in the several districts. This principle, my Lord, was acted upon at the time of my departure from the country, and should I at this moment have remained in the government thereof, I could have seen no reason whatever for departing from it. In consequence, had Mr. Talbot been totally unknown to me, except by his character, and the high rank he had borne in the King's service, I should have thought him a most eligible acquisition to this province, and on this public ground, without hesitation, have granted him 5,000 acres on the same principles that had been laid down and acted upon—this is the first part of Mr. Talbot's request. The second request of Mr. Talbot is, that these 5,000 acres may be granted in the Township of Yarmouth, in the County of Norfolk, on Lake Erie, and that the remainder of that township may be reserved for such a period as may appear advisable to government, for the purpose of his settling it, on the following specific plan, namely: that 200 acres shall be allotted to him for every family he shall establish thereon: 50 acres thereof to be granted to each family in perpetuity and the remaining 150 acres of each lot to become his property, for the expense and trouble of collecting and locating them."

Although it was found that the grant of 5,000 acres could not be made in the Township of Yarmouth, in one block, in the position desired by Col. Talbot, as large grants had already been made there to the Baby family and the Canada Company, it was made in the Township of Dunwich; while further lands were from time to time granted in that and other townships according to the plan of settlement proposed in the second part of Col. Talbot's application as stated by General Simcoe. The cultivation of hemp upon which Col. Talbot based great hopes at first, when applying for lands in Yarmouth, was abandoned as either unprofitable or unsuitable to the needs of the settlement.

It may be of interest to here mention the lands comprising the 5,000 acre grant. They were covered by two patents both dated 7th May, 1804, or two weeks less than a year after the day the Colonel landed at Port Talbot, and cut the first tree in the new settlement,—a day long after celebrated annually under the name of the Talbot anniversary as a general holiday and festival,—21st May, 1803. The lands comprised in one patent were lots 14 to 24, inclusive, and lots A and B, in the 11th Concession of Dunwich, together with broken lots 14 to 24, inclusive, and broken lots A and B, in the 12th Concession. Those covered by the other patent were lots 22, 23 and 24 in the 9th and broken lot 5 and lots 21 to 24, inclusive, and lot A, in the 10th Concession. With the exception of lot 5 in 10th Concession, they formed a solid block at and west of Port Talbot, a demesne of great natural beauty of situation and fertility of soil, where the doughty Colonel is reported, on landing with General Simcoe some years before, at the mouth of Talbot Creek, to have announced,—"Here will I roost!" (d) The isolated lot 5 in the 10th Concession appears to have succumbed to the beating of the lake storms and gone to the fishes, as it no longer appears on the map.

(d) E. Ermatinger's Life, p. 15.

General Simcoe, in the letter already quoted, proceeds to say, that the possibility had been suggested to Colonel Talbot by the representative of the government to whom he had presented his application for the grant of land, of procuring settlers in the old country, but that many reasons opposed themselves to that idea, "but should it be practicable to turn the tide of emigration, which government cannot prevent from taking place to the United States, *ultimately* to rest in this province, I beg to consider it as an object of the greatest national importance, and that will speedily fulfil the idea with which I undertook the administration of that government, under my Lord Greenville's auspices, of elevating this valuable part of His Majesty's Dominions from the degrading position of a petty factory, to be a powerful support and protection to the British Empire; in some instances, such a plan in the infancy of the government had great success, as I had the honor of pointing out to your Lordship, and Mr. Talbot, from habit, observation and nature, in my judgment, is perfectly well suited to give it a wider extent. His plan is to introduce himself amongst a large body of Welch and Scotch families, who arrived at New York in the summer of 1801, and who have temporarily fixed themselves in the interior of that State, many of whom are disgusted with the dissolute principles of the people there, (e) and feel a strong inclination to return under the government of England, but do not possess the means of purchasing land or paying the fees demanded by the Province on grants."

Whether Colonel Talbot introduced himself among the body of settlers referred to or not, it is certain that a considerable number of settlers who had been more or less permanently settled in the United States, came to the Talbot settlement (f); and that

---

(e) Governor Simcoe has been charged with undue hatred against the United States. Be this as it may, it seems to have been part of his policy to encourage the repatriation of British families from that country. See extracts from Travels of the Duke de la Rochefoucault Liancourt, published in Gourlay's Statistics of Upper Canada, Vol. 2, p. 142.

(f) According to a list of settlers on Talbot Road attested by M. Burwell, M.P., in 1817 appearing in Gourlay's Statistics of Upper Canada, Vol. 1, p. 352, out of 25 settlers therein named, 11 were natives of the United States; all of whom came in before or during the war of 1812, and many of whose descendants are still resident here.

in many cases they found it difficult to pay even the fees required to take up their patents from the Provincial Government after Colonel Talbot had assigned them their lands, (*g*) a fact which caused some conflict between the Colonel and the Provincial Government. Indeed his difficulties with the government officials at York necessitated the Colonel's repairing occasionally to England, where on all occasions he seems to have gained the ear of the Home Government and succeeded in retaining the authority assumed by him in the settlement, an authority more extensive and independent than that of any other individual in the country—an authority too, which it is now generally admitted was wisely administered in the interests of the settlers and the country generally.

In his memorial to the Secretary of State for the Colonies written in 1822, and appearing among the documents published by order of parliament in 1836, Colonel Talbot names 23 townships as then composing "the whole of what is at present called the Talbot settlement," which he goes on to say, "has now become the most compact and flourishing settlement in Upper Canada, containing as it does, a population of at least 12,000 souls, and establishing an uninterrupted communication between the Eastern and Western extremities of Lake Erie, and the settlements to the Northward." (*h*)

From the return published in the appendix of the Journal of the House of Assembly for 1836, it appears that the lands placed in the hands of the Hon. Thomas Talbot, under orders in Council and orders from the Lieut. Governor for the time being amounted to 518,000 acres, lying in 28 townships, the population thereof being estimated in 1831 at nearly 40,000. By a statement given by Colonel Talbot to Mrs. Jameson, the authoress, in 1837, the acreage then settled by him had risen to 650,000 acres, of which 98,700 were cleared and cultivated, while the population had increased to 50,000. "You see!" said he gaily, "I may boast, like the Irishman in the farce, of having peopled a whole country with my own hands." (*i*)

(*g*) See Colonel Talbot's letter to the Lieut.-Governor, dated July 29, 1831, App. Journals, L. A. U. C., No. 22, p. 18.
(*h*) App. Jour. 1836 (No. 22) p. 10.
(*i*) Sketches in Canada, by Mrs. Jameson, (new edition) p. 105.

It must not be assumed that the whole of this vast tract was settled by Colonel Talbot on the original terms granted him, viz. 150 of every 200 acres on which he had placed an actual settler. The Colonel had in 1820 completed the location of the lands put under his direction by virtue of orders from His Majesty's Government in England, by placing settlers upon 50 acres for every two hundred (*j*), and obtained a right of pre-emption of 100 acres additional for each of his settlers, which many availed themselves of—while much of the land he afterwards settled did not come within the terms of his grant.

The conditions on which free grants were made to settlers were that the settler should clear and sow ten acres of land, build a house of prescribed dimensions and open one half the road in front of his farm, all within three years. Failing this, he forfeited his claim. If he performed the conditions, he obtained fifty acres free, and the other 150 acres at $3 per acre; and a right to a further 100 acres, on payment of certain fees, was conceded also by the Provincial Government, as already stated.

The provision as to road making soon resulted in the settlement becoming noted for possessing some of the best roads in the province—notably the Talbot Road, the main artery of the settlement. Colonel Talbot's foresight in the location of grants to actual settlers and the relegation of Crown and Clergy Reserves to the rear of them, as well as the duty of road-making imposed on the settlers, brought about this result; and his policy was commended by the Home authorities for general adoption by the Provincial Government, (*k*) who had indeed already endeavored to introduce his mode of settlement generally throughout the Province, according to the Colonel's statement contained in the memorial sent by him to the Secretary of State for the Colonies in 1822, already referred to. A perusal of the dispatches and other documents published in 1836 leads to the conclusion that Colonel Talbot's policy generally, as to the opening up of the Country, commended itself to the Home Government, and it is fair to assume that the influence which the

---

(*j*) See letter from Col. Talbot to Sir Peregrine Maitland of 25th March, 1820. App. Journals 1836.
(*k*) See Lord Bathurst's dispatch of 9th April, 1822, App. Journals, 1836, (No. 22,) p. 9.

Colonel was able to bring to bear to overcome the opposition of the Provincial Government was the result of a proper appreciation by the Home authorities of the situation, rather than of any family or other influence—a recognition of the fact that the Talbot settlement was advancing in a manner unexcelled in any part of the province.

The Crown and Clergy Reserves, however, though relegated to the rear, were long a source of complaint, as impeding the improvement of the country. (*l*) But time has gradually effaced this grievance.

The manner in which the land transactions of the settlement were recorded by Colonel Talbot in early days, has been the subject of much comment. It certainly possessed the merit of simplicity, resembling in some respects the Torrens system of land transfer now in force in certain parts of the province. The permanency, which is one of the characteristics of the latter system, was not however so scrupulously provided for in the Colonel's simple method—indeed permanency of title could not of necessity obtain, where the performance of settlement duties was the chief condition, until those duties had been performed as well as the necessary fees paid, entitling the settler to obtain his patent. Until the settlement duties were performed, the settler's title rested on a simple entry in pencil of his name on his lot by the Colonel upon the map kept by him at Port Talbot. If he deserted his land or failed in the performance of his duties, his name was subject to erasure by the Colonel's rubber, and its place to be taken by that of some other more deserving settler. When his settlement duties were performed, the settler obtained from the Colonel a certificate to that effect, entitling him, on payment of the prescribed fees at York, to obtain his patent from the government.

Simple as this method was, and liable to abuse in the hands of one of a dishonorable or unjust character, to the credit of Col.

(*l*) Among the reports sent to Gourlay in answer to questions submitted by him to the various townships in 1817, are those from the townships in the present County of Elgin, everyone of which winds up with a complaint as to non-resident lands and crown reserves retarding settlement. These reports were adopted at meetings of the principal settlers of each township, and present many interesting facts and statistics. Unfortunately the book in which they are preserved is now out of print—tho' a copy remains in the Legislative Library at Toronto—Gourlay's Statistical Account of Upper Canada published in 1822.

Talbot be it said, that no abuses are recorded, no unjustice appears ever to have been done. The settlers generally had confidence in the Colonel's integrity, and found that their confidence was not misplaced. Where their duties were reasonably performed they obtained their certificates; but, difficult as no doubt were found the performance of these simple duties of building a small log house, making half the road in front and clearing and sowing ten acres of land, within three years, the settlers often found it more difficult to obtain the small sum of money necessary to enable them to take out their patents, and, having implicit confidence in the integrity of Colonel Talbot, and the potency of his certificate, they often left these patents slumbering in the pigeon holes at York for long periods—insomuch that the Provincial Government at one time complained that upwards of 5,000 deeds remained to be taken out by the settlers located under the superintendence of Colonel Talbot. (*m*)

The Colonel soon after establishing himself at Port Talbot found that he had some rough customers to deal with, who would not hesitate to employ physical force, or even weapons, to enforce their demands or take revenge for their disappointment, in case these demands were denied them. As a precautionery measure therefore, he conducted his land business through a window, a moveable pane of glass in which afforded a convenient opening for communication with the visitor without. Jeffrey Hunter, the faithful attendant of the Colonel, handed down the maps. The laconic "Well, what do you want?" with which the Colonel opened the interview, and the "Jeffrey, set on the dogs!" with which he is said to have closed an unsatisfactory one, have become historical expressions.

The wisdom of placing within the reach of one man 150 acres of the public domain for every 50 acres settled by him would no doubt now provoke much opposition. This is not the place to enter into a discussion of the question, which has been more or less discussed in connection with our northwest colonization companies of recent date; yet it may not be out of place to point to the beneficial results of an early and evenly distributed settle-

---

(*m*) See Letter of Lord Goderich to Sir J. Colborne dated 5th February, 1831. App. Journals, 1836, Vol. 1, p. 18. See also Col. Talbot's reply to Sir J. Colborne, dated July 29, 1831, at same page.

ment of this fine district and to the fact that elsewhere large tracts,—whole townships in some cases,—were by the Provincial authorities granted to individuals, as well as to the Canada Company, and that such tracts were allowed in many cases to remain undeveloped until the demand for new territory raised the price to a profitable one for the owner. That settlers themselves had a preference for the Talbot settlement, even with the limited grants given them there, to settling in other districts where large grants could be had, is indicated by the public documents already referred to, particularly that signed by Chief Justice Powell. (n) Either that was the reason of their "flocking" (as Chief Justice Powell termed it) to the Talbot settlement, or else the other desirable lands of the Province had been so disposed of to individuals or corporations as to be practically unavailable for settlement. So far as Colonel Talbot was himself concerned, the opinion has been expressed that he could have bought all the land he acquired, at the time he obtained his concession from the government, or later, for the amount he afterwards expended in settling it.

During the war of 1812-15 the settlement suffered at the hands of American marauders and their sympathisers on this side of the line, some of whom visited Port Talbot and destroyed Colonel Talbot's mill, the only one at that time in the settlement. The Colonel tells the story briefly himself, in his memorial to the Secretary of State already referred to, as follows:—

"That so early as the breaking out of the late war with the United States of America, your memorialist had conquered the principal difficulties which obstruct the growth of new settlements, and as the produce of lands sold at a fair price, your memoralist had a reasonable prospect of being rewarded for his long and vigorous executions, and an expense of upwards of £15,000. That from the character of the Talbot settlement and the principles of loyalty inculcated amongst its inhabitants it became peculiarly obnoxious to the enemy and the more so as your memorialist during the war commanded the militia of the London and Western districts and infused into them the spirit of his own settlers; two expeditions were therefore sent against Port Talbot, by which the settlement was nearly ruined. That

---

n) App. Journals, 1836 No. 22, p. 13.

your memorialist returning to Port Talbot on the restoration of peace, found a large farm which he had cleared and brought into cultivation, completely laid waste by the enemy, his grist and saw mills, erected by him at a very heavy expense for the accomodation of the surrounding settlers, burnt to the ground—all his effects carried off or destroyed, and his people reduced to the utmost distress and poverty. Nevertheless he did not despair, but diligently set himself to repair the damages he had sustained in the best manner he was able." (o)

The buildings of Colonel Burwell, near Port Talbot were among those burnt on this occasion, the Colonel (Burwell himself) having been carried off as a prisoner on a former occasion. (p)

Two months later (Nov. 1814) the work of destruction in the settlement and as far East as the Grand River, was almost completed, so far as mills and produce were concerned, by a raid made by a force of Kentuckians and Indians under General McArthur, who entered the Country with the avowed purpose of destroying all mills, to cut off supplies from the British forces. They proceeded from the Detroit to the Grand River, returning by way of the Talbot Road, pillaging the settlers, but allowing three mills in the Long Point Country to escape them in their rapid retreat. (q)

These reverses however were not allowed long to check the prosperity of the settlement, and after the close of the war mills were soon erected in St. Thomas and elsewhere throughout the settlement, to once more take the place of the rough wooden beetle and mortar in which the grain of the earlier pioneers was pounded into coarse flour.

The militia of the settlement, who rendered excellent service in this war as well as in the rebellion of 1837, were, of necessity, but poorly trained and equipped. Indeed there could have been no training at all previous to the war of 1812; when however a number of the Talbot militia were at the capture of Detroit by General Brock, and rendered service also on the Niagara frontier.

(o) App. Journal, 1836, (No. 22) p. 10.
(p) See dispatch of Lt. General Drummond, dated Sept. 19th, 1814, Canadian Archives C. 685, p. 208, Michigan Pioneer, &c. Coll Vol, 15 p. 652.
(q) See dispatches of Capt. Bostwick, dated 3rd Nov. 1814, Mr. Chambers 10th Nov. 1814 and Col. Talbot, Can. Archives c. 686, 139, 187, 677, Mich. P. and H. Coll, vol. 15 pp. 659, 667, 677.

Subsequently an annual training day was appointed—the King's birthday, 4th June,—when the militia gathered by regiments and performed such evolutions as their meagre opportunities for discipline would allow, finishing the day by toasting the King, and much jollity. Rough and undisciplined as they were, the militia of those early days stood the test of active service in a manner which drew enconiums from the highest military authorities, and went through hardships, cold and privation, in defence of their country, which seem well nigh incredible in the present comfortable, peaceful times.

"The first improvement in this settlement," says an old settler (r) speaking of the settlement along Talbot Road, "was in 1810. In 1812 the Americans declared war against Great Britain, and Canada was the theatre of their operations; so that improvement in the settlement was suspended for three years, which was a trying time for empty purses and lonely women, while the husbands were on duty to protect a home that was yet in embryo. Yet the thought of that home carried to the heart a thrill of pleasure which the wealthy cannot enjoy, for the reason that anticipation stimulated to action for years, or until the object was obtained, whereas easily acquired possession often soon cloys, so that the gratification anticipated is of short duration."—A wholesome truth is here somewhat obscured by wealth of language. The narrator proceeds: "The first act of a settler was with axe in hand to select a spot on which to erect a shanty; then felling the huge trees to a circumference that others could not reach the building when erected; then the timber had to be cut piled and burned to form a starting point for further improvement. The shanties were uniformly built of logs with elm bark for roof and floor. Then came the furniture which was invariably of home manufacture. The bedstead was made of poles with bark taken off and basswood bark for bedcord, and the tools for its construction were an axe and an auger. The table leaf was made from a piece of wood two inches thick, split from the centre of a large log, and holes made with a two inch auger to receive the legs; the seats were tripods, the material and workmanship the same as the table. Then cradles were ready for use by putting rockers to a sap-trough. I knew one

---

(r) Garrett Oakes' "Tales of a Pioneer" in the London *Free Press.*

family where the same sap-trough served to rock four of their babes in succession. The mortar was indispensable in each family. This article was made by cutting a log three feet long and 15 inches in diameter. The log then stood on end and a fire kept burning in the centre till it formed a bowl-shaped concavity to hold ten or twelve quarts. Into this a quart of corn was put and with a heavy wooden pestle pounded to the required degree of fineness, which process had to be repeated morning noon and night—or go without the indispensable johnny cake."

The settler whose remarks have been just quoted gives the prices of goods during the early days of the settlement, when there was no store west of Long Point and but one there;—established in 1807 : "Broadcloth $20 per yard; printed cottons, $1 ; steam loom cottons, $1; brass buttons a York Shilling each ; pins, 50 cents a paper ; green tea, $2 per lb; tobacco, $1 ; nutmegs, 25c. each ; board nails, 25c. per lb; shingle nails, 30c. ; 7x9 glass, 25c. a light; and every other article in proportion" Taking the long journey to Port Ryerse into account as well as the prices, one wonders that the merchant had any customers from this district—but necessity compelled, and we may only hope that the nutmegs did not turn out to be of the manufactured wooden variety, when brought home ! " During the war," we are told, nearly all the settlers had to go to Port Ryerse for their salt, pay $12 a bushel for it and carry it home on their backs. In the winter of 1813 I went to Long Point and paid $6 for 28 pounds, a neighbour offering to take it home in his sleigh. He staid over night on the road, but left his load exposed, so that a cow destroyed the salt, killed herself, and caused me to return to replace the loss. This necessitated two hundred miles of travel on foot, and $12 in cash, to realize 28 pounds of salt. During an unusual scarcity a pedlar came with a horse load. I took fourteen pounds for which I paid $8. Two of my neighbours, David Brush and Moses Rice, went to Hamilton and paid $75 for a barrel, and, allowing for their time, expenses and team, it cost them $100. But, a few days after, peace was proclaimed, and in a short time salt could be had at Port Ryerse for $12 a barrel. " A settler who could be accounted "worth his salt " in those days must have been considered an acquisition indeed to the community !

Stores were, before the lapse of many years, however, opened nearer home, in St. Thomas and elsewhere in the settlement, making the comforts of life more accessible and less costly than in the earliest days. The hardships, the privations, the discomforts, of those earliest and even later days were very great and real, though borne with great cheerfulness. Bad roads, or none at all, scarcity of everything, except fuel and perhaps game, poor clothing, rude huts, rather than houses, the wolf literally at the door, or howling near it, every night—such seem to have been the common lot of all the first settlers. Mrs. Amelia Harris in her memoirs (r) of early life at Long Point tells how by day the men took their cow with them to the woods to browse upon the branches of the trees they were felling, at night fastening her to the door latch of the house to prevent her falling a prey to prowling wolves. Sheep were unknown in the Talbot settlement during its first ten or twenty years, flax forming the staple material for clothing. The climate was quite as rigorous—if not more so—then as now,—yet the hardy settlers battled with the forest and defied the frost king, despite the lack of woollen garments and other things accounted luxuries then—necessaries now.

The rude ox-team dragging a pole split at the further end and parted in shape of a V, a board nailed across to hold the load, kept in place by wooden pins—this rough team and carriage of the early settlers has given place to the best of horses, wagons and carriages, the express train, the electric train, the pneumatic tired bicycle, of the present day—all within less than a century. Macadamized roads, paved streets, steel railways, have taken the place of the primitive bridle paths and rough corduroy roads: gas, coal oil and electric lights, the pine knot and tallow-dip. The sickle, with which the early pioneers reaped among the stumps of the freshly felled forest trees, gave place to the scythe and the cradle, they in turn to the mowing and reaping machines, they, through various stages of developement, to the present self-binders,—and this within the memory of living men who have used them all. Few, very few, of the original log houses and outbuildings remain. In their place we now see on every side handsome, slate roofed, brick residences, mammoth barns with

---

(r) See Ryerson's Loyalists of America Vol. 2, p. 235.

stone basements, in which cattle are housed with far better protection from the weather than the early farmers and their families enjoyed. Hundreds of acres of smiling fields, only too thoroughly cleared of forest trees, waving with golden grain or freshly worked with modern machinery, or green in pasture, meet the eye everywhere throughout the country, where once the hardy pioneer hewed out with his axe a few acres from the all embracing forest, to raise the means of sustenance—his descendants now perhaps burning imported coal in their houses, so valuable and scarce has wood become. Shall those whose lives may span the next century witness advances and changes greater than these?

In the early years of the Talbot Settlement the Courts for the London District which embraced a large portion of the settlement were held at Turkey Point, or more strictly speaking at the "Town of Charlotteville," (s) on the high land overlooking the point. The Township of Charlotteville was not one of those settled by Colonel Talbot, but formed part of what was known as the Long Point settlement. The Court House having been destroyed by fire, a statute passed in 1815, (t) authorized the removal of the District Courts to "the immediate vicinity of Tisdale's mills in the Township of Charlotteville" and a new Court House and Gaol were accordingly erected at Vittoria, which became the capital of the London District. This Court House having also fallen a prey to the flames, the Courts were ordered in 1826 to be holden "within some part of the reservation heretofore made for the site of a town, near the forks of the River Thames in the Townships of London and Westminster in the County of Middlesex, so soon as a Gaol and Court House shall be erected thereon" (u) and the same year Thomas Talbot, Mahlon Burwell, James Hamilton, Charles Ingersoll, and John Matthews, of Lobo, were appointed Commissioners to erect the buildings, were authorized to borrow £4,000 for that purpose, the Commissioners to first meet at the "Village of St. Thomas, in the County of Middlesex" on the first Monday in March, 1826, to select a President and Vice-President. (v) The Gaol and Court

---

(v) 7 Geo. 4, Cap. 14.
(s) See stat. of U.C., 41, Geo. 3, Cap. 6, (1801.)
(t) See 55th Geo., 3 Cap. 16.
(u) 7 Geo. 4 Cap. 13.

House at London were accordingly built, the Courts removed thither and a town begun—destined to be, ere many years, a large, handsome and prosperous city.

The Western part of the Talbot settlement (*w*) was judicially served by the District Courts of the Western District held at Sandwich.

Sandwich and its neighborhood had a white population along the Detroit River during the French Regime long previous to the commencement of the Talbot settlement. The Township of Sandwich as well as Romney, Mersea, Gosfield and Maidstone, was however included in what was known as the Talbot settlement in 1822 and previously (*x*) and these townships were no doubt all largely settled by, or the titles to their lands granted under the supervision of Col. Talbot. Over the vast tract of country extending from the Detroit River on the west to the Long Point settlement on the east, Colonel Talbot was practically sovereign. That it improved rapidly under his management was quite apparent from its condition at the time of his death, while now no more beautiful, thriving and populous agricultural district can be found perhaps in Canada. Its people are chiefly of English, Irish, Scotch, American, French and German descent, the French in the west, the Germans scattered through Aldborough and some other townships. The district now contains considerably above 300,000, including three prosperous cities, some half dozen towns and innumerable thriving villages. Its aggregate wealth is great.

Colonel Talbot died in his 83rd year, at London, in his own district, in 1853, on his return from a sojourn of a year or so, in Great Britain. His remains were interred in the picturesque little churchyard at Tyrconnell, where a plain but massive stone slab covers their last resting place. He never married. A considerable portion of his property was in his lifetime made over by the Colonel to his nephew, the late Lord Airey, military secretary, at the Horse Guards, who had, as Colonel Airey, resided with his

---

(*w*) The Talbot District established by Statute in 1837—must not be confused with the Talbot Settlement, as it embraced but a small portion of the settlement proper, though named no doubt in honour of the Colonel who had settled the Western Country.

(*x*) See Col. Talbot's memorial to the Secretary of State, for the Colonies app to Journ. 1836, No. 22, p. 10.

family at Port Talbot for some time, during his uncle's life. The balance of the lands and other property Colonel Talbot devised to the late George Macbeth, formerly M.P. for West Elgin.

"I have accomplished what I resolved to do—it is done," said Colonel Talbot to Mrs. Jameson in 1836, "but I would not, if any one was to offer me the universe, go through again the *horrors* I have undergone in forming this settlement. But do not imagine I repent it; I like my retirement (*y*)."

(*y*) Mrs. Jameson's Sketches in Canada, (new edition) p, 107.

Ontario Historical Society
1900.
TORONTO.

THOMAS LOCKER.
WARDEN 1852-5.

DEVELOPMENT OF THE COUNTY OF ELGIN.

BY

K. W. McKAY.

ORIGIN OF LOCAL GOVERNMENT.

It is said that Government by town meetings is the oldest form of Government in the world, and the student of ancient History is familiar with the Comitia of the Romans and the Ecclesia of the Greeks. These were popular assemblies held usually in the market place, the Roman Forum and the Greek Agora. The Government carried on in them was a more or less qualified Democracy.

The principle of the Town Meeting however, is older than Athens or Rome. Long before streets were built or fields fenced men wandered around the earth hunting for food in family parties. These were what we call Clans, and are supposed to have been the earliest form in which civil society appeared on the earth. Each Clan usually had a Chief or head man, useful more particularly as a leader in war-times. Its Civil Government, rude and disorderly enough, was in principle a pure democracy. When a Clan, instead of moving from place to place, fixed upon some spot for a permanent residence, a village grew up there surrounded by a belt of vacant land or somewhat later by a stockaded wall. The belt of land was called a "mark" and the wall was called a "tun"; afterwards the enclosed space came to be known sometimes as a "mark" and sometimes as a "tun" or town, and in England the latter name prevailed. It was customary to call them by their clan names. Town names of this sort are to be found all over England, and point us back to a time when each was the stationary home of a Clan. These old English towns had their Tungemot or Town Meetings in which By-Laws were made and other important business transacted. The principal officers were the Reeve, the Beadle and the Tithing Man or petty Constable. At first these officers were elected by the people, but after awhile as great lords usurped jurisdiction over the land, the Lord Stewart or Bailiff came to supercede the

Reeve or Beadle. After the Norman Conquest, the Townships, thus brought under the sway of great Lords, came to be generally known by the French name of "Manor" or dwelling places. When the taxes imposed by the Lords became excessive, the people rebelled with the result that this issue has been tried over and over again in every Country, and in every age, with various results. How much the taxes shall be, and who is to decide how much they shall be, are always questions of the greatest importance. A very large part of what has been done in the way of making history has been to settle these questions, whether by discussion or by blows, whether in Council Chambers or on the battle field.

After the English had been converted to Christianity, local Churches were gradually set up all over the Country, and districts called parishes were assigned for the administrations of the Priests. The Parish generally coincided in area with the Township, and in the course of the Thirteenth Century we find that the Parish had acquired the right of taxing itself for Church purposes. Money needed for the Church was supplied in the form of Church rates voted by the ratepayers, at the vestry meetings. The officers of the Parish were the Constable, the Bailiff and the Vestry Clerks, the Beadle, the Way-Wardens or Surveyors of Highways, and the Hay-wards or Fence-viewers, and common drivers or Collector of Taxes, and at the beginning of the Seventeenth Century Overseers of the Poor were added. There were also Church Wardens, usually two for each Parish; whose duties were primarily the care of the Church property, assessing the rates, and calling the vestry meetings. The officers were all elected by the ratepayers.

In addition to the Parish or Township, we find upon examination that a map of England shews the Country to be divided into Counties. We have seen how the Clan, when it became stationary was established as a Town or Township, and in these early times Clans were generally united more closely into tribes, made up of a number of clans or family groups. The names of the tribes were applied first to the people and afterwards to the land they occupied. A few of the oldest county names in England still shew this plainly, for example Middlesex was originally occupied by the Middle Saxons. Each tribe had its leader whose title was "Ealdorman," or elderman, and as they increased in influence they took the title of kings. The little kingdoms coincided sometimes with a single shire, sometimes with two or more shires. The Shire was governed by the Shire Mote which was a representative body. Lords of Lands, including Abbots and Priors, attended it, as well as the Reeve and four select men from each Township. As the cities and boroughs grew into importance they sent representative Burgers to these meetings. This Shire Mote was both a Legislative body and a Court of Justice. After the Norman Conquest the Shire began to be called by the French name County because of its similarity to the small pieces of Territory in that Country governed by Counts. The officers of the Shire Mote were the Shire Reeve or Sheriff, who was at first elected by the people and held office for life, but who was afterwards appointed by the King for a term of one year. The Coroner or "Crowner" was especially the Crown officer of the Court, and the Justice of the Peace. In 1362 the Justices of the Peace in each County were authorized to hold a Court four times a year.

The origin of municipal institutions in this country is due to the people who first came from England to America. They were dissatisfied with the way Church affairs were carried on in the Old Country, and were desirous of establishing a reform, whereby members of the congregation should have more voice than formerly in the Church government. It was owing to their inability to secure a reform of this nature that they crossed the ocean, settled in groups, and built their houses near together so that they could all go to the same Church. Thus a Parish, which for municipal purposes is called a Township, was formed and consisted of as many farms as were within convenient distance from the meeting house. Around the meeting house a village gradually sprang up with the customary tavern, store and town hall.

A Township, taken as a whole, and in relation to the government of the country, may be looked upon as an individual who obeys the Government, not because he is inferior to or that he is less capable than his neighbor for governing matters, but because he acknowledges the utility of an association with his fellowmen, and because he knows that no such association can exist without a regulating force. As the Townships increased in number, they became a part of larger districts called counties, without which a system of united self government would be far from complete.

In 1635 the first County was established in Massachussetts as a judicial district with its Court House, Gaol and Sheriff. The early English settlers were used to a County as a district for the Administration of Justice, and they brought with them Coroners, Sheriffs and Quarter Sessions. In Virginia a different county system was introduced. There was an insurmountable distinction between the owners of plantations and the men and women who had been indentured "white service." An aristocratic type of society was largely developed in Virginia, as readily as the democratic type was developed in New England.

In Virginia the system was that of the English Parish, with its Church Warden and Clerk, and the Vestry composed of twelve chosen men elected by the people of the Parish. The difference between the New England Township and the Virginia Parish in respect of self-government was quite plain: in New England the Township was the unit of the representation of the Colonial Legislature; in Virginia not the Parish, but the County was the unit of representation. The conditions which made the New England Town Meeting were absent, the only alternative was a kind of representative government and for this the County was a small enough area. There were usually in each County eight Justices of the Peace, and their Court was a counterpart of the Quarter Sessions. In addition to the Administration of Justice these Courts superintended the construction and repair of highways and bridges, and for this purpose divided the County into precincts, appointing annually for each precinct a highway surveyor. The first representative government in America was established in Virginia. In 1619 the colonists secured the appointment of a Governor and Council in England, and there was added a general assembly composed of two burgesses from each plantation or settlement elected by the inhabitants: this assembly met for the first time in the Church at Jamestown on 30th July, 1619. In 1634 when the Counties were re-organized the Burgesses sat for Counties. This system of Government was continued until long after the war of independence.

CANADA.

The development of Canada as the abode of civilization was not so rapid as that of her sister country to the South, for the ruggedness of the land, the opposition of savage tribes, internecine warfare between settlers, the severity of the winter season, together with many other obstacles, offered little encouragement to early settlers.

Originally the home of several tribes of Indians, who lived by the chase, prairie-land and forest were in the same condition as they had been a thousand years before the first pioneer from the eastern world penetrated into the gloom of the forest or wended his toilsome and dangerous course along the vast water-ways that led to the interior.

The brave Jacques Cartier, with his followers, took possession of the land in the name of his sovereign, Francis I., in 1534. The following year he made another visit, entered the Gulf on St. Lawrence's Day, named gulf and great river, for this reason, the St. Lawrence, sailed up to the Indian village Stadacona, (Quebec) and continuing his voyage reached another Indian village, called Hochelaga, which he named Mount Royal (Montreal). Seventy years afterwards Champlain and Pontgrave were sent out from France to trade with the Indians in furs, and subsequently, from a favorable representation of the fertility and beauty of the new country, French colonists were induced to immigrate. Several families arrived in New France, as it was then called, tradesmen built houses, soldiers erected forts, and a knowledge of Christianity was imparted to the savages by French clergymen. From the colony to the south, some English traders came and in consequence of wars at different times between England and France and between the English Colonies and the Mother Country, the early history of Canada is one of much bloodshed. Indian tribes sided with both nationalties in the country and frightful atrocities were committed on either side. In 1713, the treaty of Utrecht gave Acadia (Novia Scotia), New Foundland and Hudson Bay Territory to England, leaving

Canada, Cape Breton and Louisiana to France. About this time Quebec had a population of 7,000, Montreal 2,000, and the whole of Canada about 25,000. Trading posts were established in the west on the shores of the lakes, the principal being Kingston, Newark (Niagara), and Detroit.

QUEBEC--1763 to 1788.

By the Treaty of Paris signed on February 10th, 1763, Canada passed under British rule. In the month of October following the treaty, a proclamation was published under the great seal of Great Britian for erecting four new Civil Governments, those of Quebec, East Florida, West Florida and Granada, in the countries and islands in America which had been ceded by the definite treaty. During the interval from the capitulation of Montreal in 1760, to the conclusion of peace between the two mother countries in 1763, Canada was held under occupation by British troops. General Murray, with his headquarters at Quebec, was the chief officer over the colony. The affairs of the Country were regulated by a Council composed of military officers.

On the 21st of November, 1763, Captain James Murray was appointed Captain General and Governor-in-Chief of the Province of Quebec by Royal Commission. From the wording of the proclamation and commission it appears to have been His Majesty's intention with respect to the Province of Quebec, to assimilate the laws and government of it, to those of the other American Colonies and Provinces, which were under His Majesty's immediate government, and not to continue the Municipal laws and customs by which the conquered people had been here-to-fore governed, any further than as those laws might be necessary to the preservation of their property. This was found to be impracticable as the people had been accustomed to the French laws since 1663. Instead of a complete introduction of the English laws, a compromise was adopted. In criminal cases, Trial by Jury, and English Legal forms were established; in civil cases that effected property and inheritance, the ancient laws of the Colony were allowed to have force, but a considerable period, upwards of fourteen years, elapsed before any definite constitution or real settled modes of administration of laws can be said to have been introduced.

In 1774 when Sir Guy Carleton, the successor of General Murray, was Governor of the Colony, the Quebec Act was passed which provied for the appointment of a Council for the affairs of the Province of Quebec to consist of persons resident therein, not exceeding twenty-three or less than seventeen to be appointed by the King. This Council had the power to make ordinances for the peace, welfare and good government of the Province with the consent of the Governor. Every ordinance passed had to be transmitted to England for the approval of the King.

In 1788, under the authority of two Acts passed by the Legislative Council, Lord Dorchester, Governor, by proclamation issued on the 24th day of July, 1788, divided the Province of Quebec into five districts. The two most westerly districts were called Nassau and Hesse. In the words of the Proclamation Nassau was bounded "on the East by the North and South Line intersecting the mouth of the river now called Trent, discharging itself from the West into the Bay of Quinte, and extending so far Westerly as to a North and South line intersecting the extreme projection of Long Point into the Lake Erie on the Northerly side of the said Lake Erie."

The District of Hesse was to "comprehend all the residue of our said Province in the Western or inland parts thereof, of the entire breadth thereof from the Southerly to the Northerly boundary of the same."

THE DISTRICT OF HESSE.—1788 to 1791

The formation of the District of Hesse is the first recognition of the necessity of some system of administration of justice in what is now Western Ontario. On the day the proclamation forming the District was issued the following officers were appointed therefor:—Justices of the Court of Common Pleas, Duperon Baby, Alexander McKee and William Robertson. There were also eight Justices of the Peace, a Sheriff named

Gregor McGregor, a Clerk of the Court of Common Pleas, a Clerk of the Peace and Sessions of the Peace, Thomas Smith, Esq.

At this time the District of Hesse comprehended a very large and undefined territory; the only inhabitants were in the settlements around Detroit. These were computed at about 4,000. The public buildings at Detroit were the barracks, government house, council house where the Indians delivered their speeches, and other buildings connected with the fort and naval dock yard.

In September, 1789, an order was issued from Quebec to the board of Justices in the District of Hesse, defining the lands for settlement in Canada, " beginning at the Western boundary of the last purchase made by the Crown from the Indians, West of Niagara,(which Western boundary commenced at the mouth of the Barlow or Orwell River, now known as the Catfish Creek emptying into Lake Erie at Port Bruce; thence up a line North sixteen degrees West. This line, when produced as directed, is very near the location, if not exactly on the Western Town Line of Dorchester hereafter referred to in the formation of the County of Norfolk in 1792 as the Western boundry thereof.) Then " extending along the whole of the border of Lake Erie to the Straits of Detroit up to such distance towards Lake Huron and to such depth from the shore as they might deem expedient." These were to be surveyed and parcelled out for the accomodation of emigrant loyalists and other settlers, but before any part could be granted to individuals the whole had to be ceded to the Crown by the Indians. After this had been done the magistrates were authorized to select the proper site for a country town for the district. A situation opposite the island of Bois Blanc was recommended as the best, and for the purpose of deciding this the Magistrates were ordered to consult with the officers of the Militia and other English inhabitants. After the town site had been decided upon, the Surveyor of the District was to lay out the Townships and proceed to receive applications and issue certificates for town and farm lots. Those who already occupied improved farms were to receive certificates.

U. E. LOYALISTS.

As soon as the struggle had ended in the old Colonies by

their successful assertion of independence a vast migration of Loyalists took place into Canada, These people, who had been accustomed to the exercise of the electoreal privilege, joined with those of their countrymen who had previously settled there in demanding a modification of the Quebec Act, and the establishment of a Local Legislature. This resulted in the passage of the Constitutional Act, being 31, George III, chapter 31, by which representative institutions were conferred and the whole Province divided into two, with the designation of Upper and Lower Canada, now known as the Provinces of Ontario and Quebec.

WESTERN DISTRICT—1792 to 1798.

In July, 1792, Governor Simcoe by proclamation issued from the Government House of Kingston, under the authority of the Constitutional Act, divided the Province into nineteen counties. The Sixteenth, or County or Norfolk, was "bounded on the North and East by the County of Lincoln, and the River La Tranche now called the Thames. (The Eastern boundary was the Grand River which formed the Western boundary of the first and fourth ridings of the County of Lincoln.) On the South side by the Lake Erie until it meets the Barlue to be called the Orwell River," (now known as the Catfish Creek emptying into the lake at Port Bruce,) " thence up a line North sixteen degrees West until it intersects the river La Tranche or Thames."; "thence up the said river until it meets the North-West boundary of the West Riding of the County of York." This line from the mouth of the Orwell river, when produced as described, is very near the location, if not exactly on the Western Town-line of the Townships of North and South Dorchester The Seventeenth, or County of Suffolk, was bounded on the East by the County of Norfolk ; on the South by Lake Erie and until it meets the carrying place from the Point au Pins unto the Thames ; on the West by the said carrying place, thence up the said River Thames until it meets the North-West boundary of the County of Norfolk." This placed the territory now known as the Townships of Malahide, Dorchester and Bayham in the County of Norfolk ; the remainder of the present County formed part of the County of Suffolk.

In this division of the Province into Counties, but very little attention seems to have been paid to the boundaries of the four districts into which the Province had been already divided. If we consider the circumstances that no surveys had been made in the District of Hesse, except in the neighborhood of Detroit, and the fact that the greater part of the country on both sides of the Grand River was thickly populated by Indians, it was evidently the intention to divide the District of Hesse into four Counties, namely, Norfolk, Suffolk, Essex and Kent; the three first occupying all the territory South of the Thames. The County of Kent occupying all of the country not being territories of the Indians not already included in any of the other counties extending Northward to the Hudson Bay, and Southward of the said line to the utmost extent of the country known by the name of Canada.

For the purpose of representation the fourth riding of the County of Lincoln which was bounded on the East by the Niagara River, on the South by Lake Erie, on the West by the Grand River or Ouse, and on the North by the Chippawa or Welland River and the road leading from the forks of the Welland to the Grand River, was united with the County of Norfolk for the purpose of sending one representative to the House of Assembly. The County of Suffolk and the County of Essex were also joined together for the same purpose.

The first session of the first Provincial Parliament was convened at Niagara on the 17th day of September, 1792. The session lasted twenty-eight days. Eight Acts were passed; the first "to introduce English law as the rule for decision in all matters of controversy relative to law and civil rights." The second "to establish trials by Jury"; the third, "to establish the use of the Winchester measure and a standard for other weights and measures"; the fourth, "to abolish all summary proceedings in Courts of Common Pleas in actions under ten pounds sterling"; the fifth, "an Act to prevent accidents by fire"; sixth, "for the more easy pay and speedy recovery of small debts"; seventh, "to regulate the tolls to be taken in mills" and the eighth "for building a gaol and court house in every district within the Province, and for altering the names of the Districts."

The District named Hesse was hereafter called the Western

District. Section 13 of this Act enacted that the gaol and court house for the Western District should be built in the manner set forth, and as near the present Court House as conveniently may be. This was at Detroit.

The first Act of the Second Session of the first Parliament was "for the better regulation of the militia." The second was an Act "to provide for the nomination and appointment of parish and town officers." This Act provided that "any two of His Majesty's Justices of the Peace acting within the Division in which any parish, township, reputed township, or place may be, may issue their warrant giving eight days previous notice to the constable of such parish, township, reputed township, or place authorizing him on a day to be fixed by the said Justices in the present year, and on the first Monday in the month of March in every ensuing year, to assemble the inhabitant householders, paying or liable to pay to any public assessment or rate of such parish, township, reputed township, or place, in the parish church or chapel or in some convenient place within the said parish * * for the purpose of choosing and nominating the parish or town officers hereinafter mentioned, to serve in their respective offices for the year next ensuing, at which meeting the said constable shall preside." The office of constable appears to have still retained some of its ancient dignity in the estimation of the colonists. The inhabitant householders who assembled, were authorized to cnoose a Clerk of the Parish or Township, whose duty it should be "to make a true and complete list of every male and female inhabitant within the limits of the Parish or Township, and return the same to the Justices acting as aforesaid," and "to enter and record all such matters as shall relate to the said Parish, Town or Township, and shall appertain to his office." They were also authorized to choose two persons to serve as assessors, one person to serve as collector of taxes, and not less than two or more than six persons as specified in the warrant issued by the Justices, to serve as overseers of highways. The duty of these officers was "to oversee and perform such things as shall be directed by any Act to be passed touching or concerning the highways and roads," and to serve as fence viewers. They were also to choose a pound-keeper, and two persons to serve as town wardens, but, "as soon as any church was built for performance of divine service according to the use of the Church of England with a parson or minister duly appointed thereto," the householders should choose one of those wardens and the parson or minister nominate the other. The two so chosen and nominated were declared "a corporation to represent the whole inhabitants of the town or parish," and as such "may have a property in the goods or chattels of or belonging to the parish, and may prosecute, or defend in all presentments, indictments or actions for and on behalf of the inhabitants of the said parish." Persons neglecting or refusing to take the oath of office, and discharge the duties were subject to a penalty of forty shillings in each case, and the magistrates at a special Sessions, could name one or more persons to fill the positions they left vacant. The Act did not define the duty of any of these officers further than to state that the overseers should do whatever may be directed respecting the highways by any Act to be passed, and that as fence-viewers they should, upon receiving proper notice view and determine upon the height and sufficiency of any fence "conformably to any resolutions that may be agreed upon" at the meeting so held. And the pound-keeper was authorized to impound all cattle found trespassing upon any land properly fenced, and any stallion of more than one year old that may be found roaming at large. The same Act authorized the Magistrates at Quarter Sessions to appoint a high constable for each District annually, and constables for each Township.

If the Township did not contain 30 inhabitants it was not lawful for the Justices to issue their warrant calling a meeting therein, and said Township was joined to the Township adjacent thereto that contained the smallest number of inhabitants.

The system of County Government then introduced was similar to that already established in the state of Virginia. Chapter 4 of the Act of this Session was to regulate the laying out and mending and keeping in repair the roads and highways in the Province.

Chapter 6 was to fix the times and places of holding the Courts of General Sessions of the Peace within the several Districts of the Province.

DEVELOPMENT OF THE COUNTY. 13

Under the authority of the Act 33 Geo. III, it was directed that the Courts of Quarter Sessions of the Peace for the Western District of the Province, should commence and be holden in the Town of Detroit, and that special Sessions of the Peace should commence and be holden yearly and in every year in the Town of Michilimackinac. By Chapter 4 of the Acts passed by the first Parliament on the 3rd June, 1796 it was enacted that the Court of General Quarter Sessions of the Peace for the Western District shall commence and he holden in the Parish of Assumption, now Sandwich, in such place as may be found to be most convenient for the Magistrates of said District or the major part of them, on the second Tuesdays of the months of July, October, January and April until such time as it shall seem expedient to the Magistrates or the major part of them to remove and hold the same nearer to the Island called the Island of Bois Blanc (opposite Amherstburg,) being near the entrance to the River Detroit. The District Court for the cognizance of small cases was also at this time removed from the town of Detroit, and ordered to be held at and in the same place wherein the General Quarter Sessions were to be held. This change was necessary owing to the evacuation of Detroit by the British in 1795. The work of surveying Townships under direction of the Provincial Government was now being carried on, and during the second session of the Second Parliament, held at York in 1798, an Act was passed constituting the Township of London, Westminster, Dorchester, Yarmouth, Southwold, Dunwich, Aldborough and Delaware, to form the County of Middlesex, and also to constitute the Townships of Burford, Norwich, Dereham, Oxford upon the Thames, Blanford and Blenheim as the County of Oxford. The Townships of Rainham, Walpool Woodhouse, Charlotteville, Walsingham, Houghton, Middleton, Windham and Townsend were formed into the County of Norfolk. Section 37 of this Act enacted "that the Counties of Norfolk, Oxford and Middlesex with so much of this province as lies to the westward of the Home District and the District of Niagara, to the southward of Lake Huron and between them and a line drawn due north from a fixed boundary (where the easternmost limit of the Township of

Oxford intersects the River Thames) till it arrives at Lake Huron, be constituted to form the District of London.

DISTRICT OF LONDON—1800—1837.

ORGANIZATION.

With the promulgation by Proclamation bearing date the first day of January, 1800 of the Act passed establishing the District of London, a general commission of the Peace was issued for the said District. The following extract from the original records will shew the manner in which the Commission was received, the District organized, and a General Quarter Sessions of the Peace established:—

DISTRICT OF LONDON, UPPER CANADA.

On the first day of April, in the year of our Lord one thousand eight hundred, and about noon on the same day, a packet was delivered to me by Samuel Ryerse, Esquire, which packet contained a General Commission of the Peace for the District of London, dated at York the first day of January, one thousand eight hundred. And in and by the said Commission of the Peace the following Honorable Gentlemen and Gentlemen are appointed to be His Majesty's Justices of the Peace, in and for the District of London, that is to say, the Honorable John Elmsley, the Honorable Peter Russell, the Honorable Phineas Shaw, the Honorable James Baby, the Honorable Alexander Grant, the Honorable John McGill, the Honorable David William Smith, the Honorable William Dummer Powell, the Honorable Henry Allcock, Samuel Ryerse, William Spurgin, Peter Teeple, Thomas Hornor, Benjamin Springer, John Backhouse, John Beemer and Wynant Williams, Esquires; also three other commissions nominating and appointing me to be Clerk of the Peace, Clerk of the District Court and Registrar of the Surrogate Courts. Also, a Commission dated at York the twelfth day of February, one thousand eight hundred, nominating and appointing Samuel Ryerse, Thomas Hornor, Esquires, and myself to be commissioners for taking the acknowledgements of recognizance or recognizances of bail or bails for the Court of King's Bench; also, Dedimus Potestatem dated at York, the first day of January, one thousand eight hundred, nominating and appointing Samuel Ryerse, William Spurgin and Peter Teeple, Esquires, to be Commissioners for administering the oaths prescribed by law to the officers of the Government.

THOMAS WELCH, C. P.

April 1st, 1800.

April 2nd, 1800.

At a meeting of the Magistrates resident in the Townships of Charlotteville and Woodhouse, who met at the house of James Munro, in Charlotteville, for the purpose of carrying into execution the intention of His Majesty's Commissioners of the Peace for the District of London, the following persons were duly sworn into office according to law, that is to say :—William Spurgin, Esquire, by Samuel Ryerse, Esquire; Samuel Ryerse, Esquire, by William Spurgin, Esquire; and Peter Teeple, Esquire, by Samuel Ryerse, Esquire, as Justices of the Peace; Thomas Welch, Esquire, by Samuel Ryerse, Esquire, as Clerk of the Peace, all between the hours of 9 and 12 o'clock in the forenoon of the same day.

THOMAS WELCH, C. P.

The aforesaid Justices then formed themselves into a special Session of the Peace.

THOMAS WELCH, C. P.

The Court of Special Sessions of the Peace opened in due form; Samuel Ryerse, Esquire in the chair.

Ordered by the Court that a Venire be made out in due form requiring and commanding the Sheriff of the District of London, to make Proclamation throughout the District, that a General Quarter Sessions of the Peace, in and for the District of London, will be holden at the house of James Munro, in Charlotteville, on Tuesday, the eighth of this present month of April, at ten o'clock in the forenoon of the same day, and to summon a jury for the said Court, which being done, the Court is adjourned to Tuesday next, at 10 o'clock a. m.

THOMAS WELCH, C. P.

DISTRICT } APRIL the 8th, 1800.
OF LONDON.
TO WIT: } The General Quarter Sessions of the Peace holden

at the house of James Munro, in Charlotteville, in and for the said District on the eighth day of April, in the fortieth year of the reign of our Sovereign Lord George III, of Great Britain, France and Ireland, King, Defender of the Faith, and so forth, and in the year of our Lord one thousand eight hundred : before the Justices of our said Lord the King, assigned to keep the Peace in the said District, and also to hear and determine divers felonies, trespasses and other misdemeanors in the said District committed, and of the Quorum.

1. Samuel Ryerse, Esquire—Chairman.
2. William Spurgin.
3. Peter Teeple.
4. John Beemer, and
5. Wynant Williams, Esquires, associate Justices attending.

JOSEPH RYERSON, ESQUIRE, Sheriff,
THOMAS WELCH, Clerk of the Peace.

GRAND INQUEST.

1. Dan Millard—Foreman.
2. Nathan B. Barnum.
3. William B. Hilton.
4. Robert Munro.
5. Silas Secord.
6. Lucas Tederick.
7. John Davis.
8. William Cope.
9. Jacob Buckner.
10. Peter Walker.
11. Phillip Force.
12. James Mathews.
13. John Gustin.

APRIL the 8th, 1800.

The Court met according to appointment or adjournment and opened in due form.

Wynant Williams and John Beemer Esquires took and subscribed the oaths subscribed by law, as Justices of the Peace, in and for the District of London, the oaths administered by Samuel Ryerse, Esquire, in open Court, between the hours of 9 and 12 o'clock in the forenoon.

William Budd Gould, gentleman, is appointed by the Court to be High Constable of the District of London, and sworn into office, according to law, in open Court: and Constables for the present year were at the same time nominated and appointed by the Court, viz. :—Moses Rice for Charlotteville, sworn in open Court. Albert Berdan, for Woodhouse, Walpole and Rainham and Crier of the Quarter Sessions and District Court, and sworn in open Court. Simon Mabee, for Walsingham, sworn in open Court, and John Muckle, junior, for Townsend and Windham, and sworn in open Court.

The Grand Jury sworn in due form, and the charge given them by the chairman.

Simon Mabee, Constable attending the Grand Jury.

APRIL, the 8th, 1800.

The Grand Jury present, the publick roads of the District as being not laid out according to law, by means whereof they are grievious and a public nuisance.

Ordered, that Juries be summoned and sworn in different parts of the District, to view and report on the grounds on which roads are required to be laid out.

Personal applications in Court for better regulations of the publick roads in different Townships, viz.:—

For Charlotteville, Dan Millard.

For Townsend and Windham, Jabez Collver, Sr.

For Woodhouse, Richard Mead.

The Court is adjourned to two o'clock p. m.

The Court met according to adjournment, and opened in due form.

Samuel Ryerse sworn into office as Surrogate, and Thomas Welch also sworn into office as Registrar of the Surrogate Court: both sworn according to law in open Court.

The Grand Jury dismissed by the Court at four o'clock p. m.

The Court is adjourned until to-morrow at ten o'clock a. m.

APRIL the 9th, 1800.

The Court met according to adjournment, and opened in due form.

1. Samuel Ryerse, Esquire, Chairman. 2. William Spurgin.
3. Peter Teeple. 4. John Beemer, and
5. Wynant Williams, Esquires, associate Justices.

Joseph Ryerson, Esquire, Sheriff.

The petition of James Munro of Charlotteville, praying to be recommended by the Court in order to obtain a License to keep a house of public entertainment at the house he now dwells at, was read in Court, and the prayer of the Petitioner granted.

The petition of Joseph Woolley of Walsingham, praying to have his Statute Labor on the highways lessened, was read in Court, and his labor on the publick roads stated by the Court, at two days for the ensuing year.

The petition of Titus Finch and others for a road, read in Court and ordered to lie on the table.

The petition of Walter Anderson of Charlotteville, praying to have his Statute Labor on the Highways lessened, was read in Court, and the prayer of the petitioner granted, stating his statute labor on the public highways at four days for the ensuing year.

ORDERED BY THE COURT

That no composition for labor on the highways for the ensuing year, be permitted within the District of London.

The Court is adjourned to Saturday next at 9 o'clock a. m

APRIL the 12th, 1800.

The Court met according to adjournment, and opened in due form.

1. William Spurgin, Esquire, in the chair. 2. Peter Teeple.
3. Wynant Williams, and 4. John Beemer, Esquires, associate Justices.

The opinion of the Court being taken, respecting Mr. Jabez Collver's papers, the Court is of opinion that with the addition of his oath if required, his ordination may be sufficiently authenticated.

The petition of sundry inhabitants of Charlotteville, praying for a road to be laid out in that Township, read in Court and ordered to lie on the table.

Nathan Bunnell Barnum, and Finlay Malcom are appointed by the Court to be each of them a keeper of a standard for weights and measures within the District of London, and the Clerk of the Peace is ordered by the Court, to notify them respectively of their appointment as soon as possible.

ORDERED BY THE COURT.

That Samuel Ryerse, Wynant Williams and John Beemer, Esquires, do act as Justices of the Court of Request, and Commissioners of Highways in and for that Division of the District of London which is composed of the Townships of Rainham, Walpole, Woodhouse and Townsend. The Courts of Request for the said Division to be holden at the house of James Clendennen in Woodhouse.

That William Spurgin and Peter Teeple, Esquires, do act as Justices of the Court of Request, and Commissioners of Highways, in and for that Division of the District of London which comprehends the Townships of Charlotteville, Walsingham, Houghton and Middleton. The Courts of Request to be holden at the dwelling house of Miden Stacy in Charlotteville.

The petition of Silas Secord and others, praying redress of grievances on account of the officers appointed in this County, particularly of the person whom the Petitioners state is appointed Deputy Sheriff; was read in Court, and ordered by the Court to be filed of record.

Dan Millard Esquire, of Charlotteville, is appointed by the Court to be Treasurer of the District of London.

The Court do resolve as follows, that is to say:

1st. That as soon as the Court can be furnished with certain information of what is allowed in the Court of Quarter Sessions for the District of Niagara for extra services performed by the Clerk of the Peace in the line of his duty.

2nd. Fees to the Town Clerks for services performed in the line of their duty.

3rd. Fees to the Pound-keepers for the services performed in the line of their duty.

4th. Fees to the Crier of the Court of Quarter Sessions for services performed in the line of his duty; the Court will proceed to take order therein accordingly.

5th. That the Court will proceed to consider and determine of the ways and means for defraying the expenses which will be incurred in procuring seals, books, etc., etc., for the several Courts of Quarter Sessions, the District Court and Surrogate Court of this District.

The Court is adjourned to the Second Tuesday in July next.

THOMAS WELCH,
Clerk of the Peace.

DISTRICT⎫ JULY 8th, 1800.
OF LONDON. ⎬
TO WIT: ⎭ The General Quarter Sessions of the Peace, holden at the House of James Munro, in Charlotteville in and for the said District on the eighth day of July, in the fortieth year of the Reign of our Sovereign, Lord George the Third, of Great Britain, France and Ireland, King, Defender of the Faith, and so forth. Before the Justices of our said Lord, the King, assigned to keep the Peace in the said District, and also to hear and determine divers felonies, trespasses and other misdemeanors in the said District committed, and of the Quorum.

The Court met according to adjournment, and opened in due form.

1. Samuel Ryerse, Esquire, Chairman. 2. William Spurgin.
3. Peter Teeple. 4. John Beemer.
5. Thomas Hornor. 6. John Backhouse,
7. and Wynant Williams, Esquires, Associate Justices.

JOSEPH RYERSON, Sheriff.

THOMAS WELCH, Clerk of the Peace.

Proclammation made in due form, and the Commission of the Peace, and the Act of Parliament for the better securing the Province against the King's enemies publickly read.

THE GRAND INQUEST.

1. Isaac Gilbert, Foreman.   8. Job Slaght, Sr.
2. Walter Anderson.   9. Philip Sovereign.
3. Robert Henderson.   10. John Culver.
4. Joseph Lemon.   11. Michael Shoaff.
5. Larrance Johnson.   12. William Dill.
6. Daniel McColl, Jr.   13. John Sovereign.
7. Abraham Powell.

Moses Rice, Constable attending the Grand Jury.

The Grand Jury sworn and their charge delivered to them in due form, by the Chairman.

John Backhouse, Esquire took and subscribed the oath prescribed by law, as one of His Majesty's Justices of the Peace for this District in open Court. Oaths administered by Samuel Ryerse, Esquire.

RULE OF COURT.

The Clerk of the Peace shall be allowed to ask, demand and receive of and from each person claiming a Bill of Indictment, the sum of Ten Shillings, lawful money of this Province, and two shillings like money for each subpœna, except in extraordinary cases where the Court may think proper to order otherwise.

The proceedings of the last April Sessions being publickly read by order of the Court, and the opinion of that session relative to the proof offered by Jabez Collver, sr., of his ordination to the Ministry of the Gospel, is protested against by Samuel Ryerse, Esquire.

Artimus Rogers is nominated and appointed by the Court to be Constable for the Township of Burford.

Hammon Lawrence is appointed by the Court to be Constable for the Township of Oxford.

Proclamation being made in due form, and the Justices of the Peace called upon to give in their record, a conviction and six shillings fine against Daniel McColl, jr., for profane swearing on the 28th day of June last.

Silas Secord appears in Court on Recognizance at suit of the King, and is discharged on paying costs.

The Court is adjourned to to-morrow at ten o'clock a. m.

JULY the 9th, 1800.

The Court met according to adjournment and opened in due form.

1. Samuel Ryerse, Esquire, Chairman.   2. William Spurgin.
3. Peter Teeple.   4. Thomas Hornor.
5. John Beemer, and   6. John Backhouse, Esquires,
Associate Justices.

JOSEPH RYERSON, ESQUIRE, SHERIFF.
THOMAS WELCH, Clerk of the Peace.

The Grand Inquest and Traverse Jurors called and dismissed by the Court.

A Report of the Road between Townsend and Windham, also in the Township of Oxford and Burford, and on Dundas street was read in Court.

ORDERED BY THE COURT.

That the Commissioners of Roads, in and for the Townships

Windham and Townsend, do proceed and lay out the above roads as soon as it can conviently be done. The said four reports being delivered to the Commissioners of roads by order of the Court.

Ordered by the Court, that John Beemer and Thomas Hornor, Esquires, do act of Justices of the Peace and Commissioners of Roads in and for the Townships of Windham and Townsend in the County of Norfolk, and also in and for the Counties of Oxford and Middlesex. And that the places for holding the Courts of Request for the above division shall be at the dwelling houses of Mordecai Sayles, in Townsend, and John Fowler in Burford alternately. And that John Backhouse, Esquire, do act as a Justice of the Peace in the Court of Request holden at the dwelling house of Moiden Stacy in Charlottevillle, and as a Commissioner of Roads for the Township of Charlotteville and Walsingham.

Hammon Lawrence, of the Township of Oxford, is appointed by Court to be a keeper of a standard for weights and measures agreeably to the Provincial Statute in that case made and provided.

The petition of Hammon Lawrence of Oxford, praying to be recommended for the purpose of obtaining a license for keeping a publick house of entertainment at the house he now dwells at, was read in Court, and the prayer of the Petitioner granted.

The petition of John Fowler of the Township of Burford, praying to be recommended for the purpose of obtaining a license to keep a publick house of entertainment at the house he now dwells at was read in Court and the prayer of the petitioner granted.

The Court is adjourned to Saturday next at three o'clock in the afternoon.

JULY the 12th, 1800.

The Court met according to adjournment and opened in due form.
1. Samuel Ryerse, Esquire, Chairman.
2. William Spurgin.
3. And Wynant Williams, Esquires Associate Justices.

JOSEPH RYERSON, ESQUIRE, Sheriff

THOMAS WELCH, Clerk of the Peace.

The Treasurer of this District is notified by the Court, he

being present in Court, that he must give bonds with good and sufficient security, (as soon as assessed rates in and for this District shall be ordered to be collected) in the penal sum of one hundred and twenty-two pounds lawful money of this Province, for the faithful discharge of the duties of his office as Treasurer.

The Court is adjourned to the second Tuesday in October next.

THOMAS WELCH, Clerk of the Peace.

DISTRICT ⎱   OCTOBER the 14th, 1800.
OF LONDON. ⎰
To WIT : The General Quarter Sessions of the Peace, holden at the house of James Munro in Charlotteville, in and for the said District, on the Fourteenth day of October, in the Fortieth year of the Reign of our Sovereign, Lord George the Third, of Great Britain, France and Ireland, King, Defender of the Faith and so forth. Before the Justices of our said Lord the King, assigned to keep the Peace in the said District, and also to hear and determine divers felonies, trespasses and other misdemeanors in the said District committed, and of the Quorum.

1. Samuel Ryerse, Esquire, Chairman; 2. William Spurgin, 3. Peter Teeple, 4. John Backhouse, 5. Thomas Hornor, and 6 John Beemer, Esquires, associate Justices.

JOSEPH RYERSON, ESQUIRE, Sheriff.

THOMAS WELCH, Clerk of the Peace.

The Court met according to adjournment and opened in due form.

Motion of Samuel Ryerse Esquire, that the Justices will nominate a Chairman, which being done, Samuel Ryerse, Esquire, was unanimously chosen.

THE GRAND INQUEST.

1. Nathaniel Landon, Foreman: 2, Justice Stephens; 3, David Parmer; 4, Josiah F. Deen; 5, Hugh Graham; 6, Samuel Baker; 7, John Fowler: 8, Charles Burch; 9, John Wells; 10, James Smiley; 11, Elijah Mudge; 12, Alexander Hoy; 13, John Mudge; 14, Roswell Matthews; 15, Reuben Dayton; 16, John Eaton ; 17, Thomas Sayles.

The Grand Jury duly sworn, and their charge delivered to them by the Chairman.

Constable attending the Grand Jury.

Motion by William Budd Gould, High Constable of the District, requesting leave to resign the office of High Constable, the Court will accept of his resignation, he continuing to serve during the present Sessions of the Peace.

The Petition of William Hambly of Woodhouse, praying for a Road to be opened on lands reserved for that use in that township.

ORDERED BY THE COURT.

That all reserves for Roads as the same are marked off in the Map of each Township within this District, be henceforward left uninclosed for the purpose of the King's Highways only.

Daniel McColl, James Munro, John McColl, Jabez Collver, jr., Nisbitt Collver, Aaron Collver, John Cullver, appeared in open Court and acknowledged Mr. Jabez Collver, sr., to be their settled Minister of a congregation of Presbyterians in the District of London.

The Court is adjourned until to-morrow at ten o'clock a. m.

OCTOBER the 15th, 1800.

The Court met according to adjournment, and opened in due form.

Samuel Ryerse, Esquire, Chairman; William Spurgin, Peter Teeple, John Backhouse, Thomas Hornor and John Beemer, Esquires, Associate Justices; Joseph Ryerson, Sheriff; Thomas Welch, Clerk of the Peace.

The Petition of Frederick Oustine of Rainham, praying to be recommended for the purpose of obtaining a license to keep a public house of entertainment at the house he now dwells at, was read in Court, and the prayer of the petitioner granted.

Dan Millard sworn in Court, to give evidence to the Grand Jury.

Ordered by the Court, that a road leading from Lake Erie to the Mills of John Backhouse, Esquire, as it is now marked and in part opened between lots number Sixteen and Seventeen, be henceforward considered and kept in repair as a public highway.

John McColl and John Coltman, sworn in Court to give evidence to the Grand Jury.

The Grand Jury having presented the Road from James Munro's to Burford.

Ordered by the Court, that the Commissioners of Highways do immediately proceed to open that part of the said road that is already laid out.

John Fowler brought before the Court by the complaint of John McColl, for selling spiritous liquors without License.

By the Court, no complaint can lie in John Fowler's case, he being considered as having authority to retail spiritous liquors.

John Davis and Luther Cooley being presented by the Grand Jury for selling spiritous liquors.

Ordered by the Court, that summonses do immediately issue for John Davis and Luther Cooley to appear at the Bar of this Court, at two o'clock on Friday next, in the afternoon, to answer to the above complaint. Artimus Rogers, Constable, is appointed to serve the above summonses.

The Court is adjourned in due form till to-morrow at ten o'clock a.m.

THOMAS WELCH, C. P.

October the 16th, 1,800.

The Court met according to adjournment, and opened in due form. The same Justices as yesterday.

Abraham Powell, sworn in Court to give evidence to the Grand Jury.

Motion of Thomas Horner, Esq., that movable stocks and whipping post be immediately erected at the expense of the District, and paid for out of the first collection of assessments for this District. Carried unanimously in the affirmative.

Samuel Ryerse, Esquire, agrees to have the same immediately erected on the above terms.

Motion of William Budd Gould, High Constable for leave of absence from the Court, to go to Murphy Creek, near Long Point on a pressing occassion. Granted.

Abraham Powell recognized in the sum of five pounds lawful money of this Province, to appear at the next Court of Quarter Sessions of the Peace for this District, to give evidence for our Lord the King, against Samuel Miles.

High Graham, recognized in the sum of five pounds, lawful money of this Province, to appear and give evidence for our Lord the King, against Luther Cooley at the next General Quarter Sessions of the Peace for this District.

David Parmer, recognized in the sum of five pounds, lawful money of this Province, to appear and give evidence for our Lord the King, against John Davis at the next General Quarter Sessions of the Peace for this District.

Silas Secord, presented by the Grand Jury, for wilful and corrupt perjury; Preceipt issued for Silas Secord to appear on the Seventeenth instant, at ten o'clock in the forenoon of the same day.

The Grand Jury dismissed by the Court.

The Court adjourned till to-morrow at ten o'clock a.m.

THOMAS WELCH, C.P.

OCTOBER the 17th, 1800.

The Court met according to adjournment and opened in due form.

1, Samuel Ryerse, Esquire, Chairman; 2, William Spurgin; 3, Peter Teeple; 4, John Backhouse, 5, Thomas Hornor, and 6, John Beemer, Esquires, Associate Justices.

JOSEPH RYERSON, ESQUIRE, Sheriff.
THOMAS WELCH, Clerk of the Peace.

Ensign John Eaton, appeared in Court and took the oath prescribed by law as a Militia Officer.

Luther Cooley being Indicted by the Grand Jury for selling spiritous liquors without License, appeared on Process and pleaded not guilty, recognized to appear at the next sessions of the Peace to prosecute his Traverse to affect himself in the sum of 40 pounds. Artimus Rogers and John Mudge in the sum of 20 pounds each.

John Davis, being indicated by the Grand Jury for selling spiritous liquors without License, appeared on process and pleaded not guilty; recognized to appear at the next sessions of the Peace, to prosecute his Traverse, to affect, himself in the sum of 40 pounds, and John McColl and Albert Berdan each in the sum of 20 pounds as his sureties.

Silas Secord, being indicated by the Grand Jury for wilful and corrupt perjury, on the 20th day of September last, appeared in Court on process, recognized to appear at the next Assizes to be holden in and for this District, himself in the sum of 100 pounds, and John McColl and Moses Rice each in the sum of 50 pounds as his securities.

Dan Millard, recognized to appear at the next Assizes to be holden in and for this District to prosecute Silas Secord on behalf of the King, himself in the sum of 100 pounds and Albert Berdan and Othniel Smith as his securities, each in the sum of 50 pounds.

Ordered by the Court, that process shall issue against Samuel Miles at the suit of the King, to be bound over in recognizance to appear at the next session of the Peace.

The Court is adjourned till to-morrow at ten o'clock a.m.

THOMAS WELCH, C.P.

OCTOBER, the 18th, 1800.

The Court met according to adjournment and opened, etc.

The Petition of Moses Rice of Charlotteville, praying to be recommended for a Tavern License. Granted.

Justices attending to-day the same as yesterday.

Bejamin Fairchild, Ensign of the Militia of Norfolk, came into Court, and took the oath of Allegiance as such.

Thomas Hornor, Esquire, with Joseph Ryerson, Esquire and Benjamin Fairchild entered into regular Recognizance, as the said Thomas Hornor being appointed by His Excellency the Lieutenant Governor, Register of Deeds, Conveyances, Wills and other Incumbrances, etc., etc., for the Counties of Oxford and Middlesex, before Samuel Ryerse, William Spurgin, Peter Teeple, John Backhouse and John Beemer, Esquires, Justices; who approved of the principal and securities. And the said Thomas Hornor was sworn into office as Registrar as aforesaid, before Samuel Ryerse, and William Spurgin and John Backhouse, Esquires. in open Court.

John Bostwick is appointed by the Court to be High Constable of the District of London.

Ordered by the Court that William Budd Gould's resignation of the office of High Constable is accepted of. And that the Clerk of the Peace do furnish him with a certificate thereof, and of his services whilst in that office.

Ordered, that the Court do meet in Special Sessions of the Peace, at the Town of Charlotteville on Monday the Third day of November next, at ten o'clock in the forenoon, to consider of ways and means for building a Gaol and Court House at the Town of Charlotteville aforesaid for the District of London.

The Court is adjourned until the day prescribed by law.

THOMAS WELCH, Clerk of the Peace.

NOVEMBER the 3rd, 1800.—Special Sessions.

The Special Sessions of the Peace met at the Town of Charlotteville according to the order of Sessions of the eighteenth of October last, the Court opened in due form.

Present in Court, William Spurgin, Peter Teeple, and John Backhouse, Esquires, Justices.

THOMAS WELCH, Clerk of the Peace.

ORDERED BY THE COURT.

That the Clerk of the Peace do publish in the name of the Court according to written orders and directions to be made out and sent him, by William Spurgin, Esquire concerning the object of this Special Session. And that a Special Sessions will be holden at this place on Monday the Tenth of this present month, in order further to proceed touching and concerning the object of this special sessions. To which time, this special sessions being adjourned in due form.

THOMAS WELCH, Clerk of the Peace.

NOVEMBER, the 10th, 1800—Special Sessions.

The Special Sessions of the Peace met according to adjournment and opened in due form.

Present in Court, Samuel Ryerse, Esquire, Chairman; Wynant Williams, William Spurgin, Peter Teeple, and John Backhouse, Esquires, Associate Justices.

THOMAS WELCH, Clerk of the Peace.

Levi Comber agrees to build a Gaol and Court House at this place for the sum of Three Hundred and Twelve Pounds Ten Shillings, lawful money of this Province, and to wait for his pay by receiving the annual interest yearly, therefor, until the District shall be able to pay the principal; mason work, brick, stone, lime, window glass, nails, spikes, locks and hinges excepted.

Ordered by the Court; that Samuel Ryerse and Wynant Williams, Esquires, be and are by this Special Sessions appointed a committee to assemble and meet at the House of the said

Samuel Ryerse, Esquire, on Saturday the Fifteenth day of this present month in order to enter into a contract in form with the said Levi Comber, to perform the said buildings; and that the Clerk of the Peace do notify each person recommended for a Tavern License, to produce the same licenses at the next General Quarter Sessions.

THOMAS WELCH, Clerk of the Peace.

NOVEMBER, the 15th, 1800.—Special Sessions.

The Special Sessions met according to appointment in Committee.

Present in Committee, Samuel Ryerse, Esquire, and Wynant Williams, Esquire, } Committee.

John Backhouse, Esquire and Peter Teeple, Esquire, } Visitors.

THOMAS WELCH, Clerk of the Peace.

Levi Comber having declined the business of the contract for building a Gaol and Court House at the Town of Charlotteville.

Ordered by the Court that the Clerk of the Peace do publish that a Special Sessions will be holden at the house of James Munro on Saturday the thirteenth day of December next, where proposals will be received by the Magistrates for the District of London, for the contract for building a Gaol and Court House at the Town of Charlotteville. A plan or plans of the said building will be produced at the time and place aforesaid for public inspection, and of the party contracting to perform the work, good and sufficient security will be required.

THOMAS WELCH, Clerk of the Peace.

DECEMBER, the 13th, 1800—Special Sessions.

The Special Sessions met according to adjournment and opened in due form.

1, Samuel Ryerse, Esquire, Chairman; 2, William Spurgin; 3, Peter Teeple; 4. Wynant Williams; and 5, John Beemer, Esquires, Associate Justices.

THOMAS WELCH, Clerk of the Peace.

No proposals being offered to the Court, of the contract for building a Goal and Court House. The following description is ordered by the Court to be published by the Clerk of the Peace, that is to say :—

Any person or persons who may be willing or inclined to

undertake to erect and complete a Gaol, on the ground laid out and set apart for that purpose, at the Town of Charlotteville in and for the District of London, are hereby desired to deliver their proposals in writing sealed, into this office, before the second Tuesday in January next, and at the General Quarter Sessions of the Peace, then to be holden in and for the District aforesaid, the lowest bidder will be employed to erect and complete the said Gaol, provided such person or persons do then and there enter into Bonds with good and sufficient security for his or their performance. The description of the said building as agreed upon by His Majesty's Justices of the Peace this day in Special Sessions of the Peace assembled at Charlotteville, in and for the District aforesaid, is as follows, that is to say:—To be built with squared logs of white oak ten inches thick, on a foundation of black walnut logs, so deep in the ground that the lower floor of the building may be below the surface of the earth. The building is to measure thirty-four by twenty feet from outside to outside, and ten feet from floor to floor, and to be divided into three rooms of twelve feet by ten each, and the remainder to be an entry, to be lined as the outsides. The partition walls to be made with squared logs six inches thick. The whole building is to be weather boarded with inch and quarter boards, not to exceed ten inches in width, and to be lapped with feather edge, and the whole building is to be lined with good two inch white oak plank to be lapped, halved or groved at each joint, and spiked with such spikes as are usually made use of for such purposes.

The building is to be covered, first with inch and quarter white oak plank, then with good shingles, the plank to be lapped with feather edge. The logs of the floors are to be squared white oak ten inches thick, and laid close together side and side, and the floors over those logs to be two inch white oak plank to be lapped, halved or groved as aforesaid. There is to be a good brick chimney in each of two of the rooms with a three feet back to each, with the customary fleer. The four doors one outside and three inside are to be made of two inch white oak, plank doubled and spiked in the usual manner; with a lock and key to each door of the usual size and strength. There are to be a window in each of the two rooms with iron grates to each window, to be more particularly described at the time of making the contract, and the whole to be completed on or before the second Tuesday in October next.

THOMAS WELCH, Clerk of the Peace.

This Special Session is adjourned till the 2nd Tuesday in January next.

THOMAS WELCH, Clerk of the Peace.

In 1801 an Act was passed which provided that the Courts of General Quarter Sessions of the Peace for the District of London should be holden in the Town of Charlotteville on the second Tuesday of the months of March, June, September and December. Charlotteville was situated in the south-west part of the Township of that name in the County of Norfolk at Turkey Point. It was sometimes called Port Norfolk, and it was here the building was erected which was used as a Court House up to the year 1816.

The foregoing proceedings of the Quarter Sessions will serve to illustrate the success that attended the organization of the District.

The following extracts of the proceedings up to September the 9th, 1809, will show the progress made by the Court as an official body, and the extent to which Townships comprising the present County of Elgin were interested.

April 14th, 1801, a Constable appears to have been necessary for the County of Middlesex, and Timothy Kilburn, of Delaware, was appointed to fill that office, during the same sessions it was ordered that the Township of Oxford and the County of Middlesex were to be a distinct division of the District, and that Thomas Ingersoll and Daniel Springer were to act as Justices of the Court of Request and Commissioners of Roads for the said division; the Court of Request to be holden alternatively at the houses of Thomas Springer of the Township of Delaware and Hammon Lawrence of the Township of Oxford.

MARCH 10th, 1803.—A memorandum shows that the Gaol, although previously ordered, had not been finished. The Grand Jury then present that it is highly necessary that there should be a publick Goal in this County for the reception of prisoners, and that the one erected on the public ground, if finished, would answer the present purpose. At this time the Courts were being held in the house of Job Lodor.

JUNE 15th, 1803.—It was decided to hold a Special Sessions to receive proposals from any person who may be willing or desirous to contract for finishing the Gaol at Turkey Point.

OCTOBER 4th, 1803.—It was proposed and agreed to have a Court House erected on the public ground at the Town of Charlotteville of the following description:—A frame building forty feet in length by twenty-six feet in width, to be two stories high the first or lower story to be ten feet between floor and ceiling, and the second or upper story to be eight feet high. The building to be erected on a foundation of white oak timber squared, the same to be sound and of sufficient thickness, the building to be shingled and to have two sufficient floors, an entry of eight feet wide to be made from the front door across one end of the lower story, from which winding stairs are to be erected to ascend to the second story, two rooms are to be partitioned off in the second or upper story, for the Juries. Nine windows are to be made in front, and ten in rear, of twenty four lights each, seven by three. The front door to be made of inch and a half plank, 6 panel, to have a good sufficient lock and key. Two windows are to be finished in the first story opposite each other, so as to afford sufficient light to the Bar, besides two windows of fifteen lights each behind the Judge or Chairman's seat. The rest of the windows are to be cased and nailed up for the present the Bar, table, Justices' seat, benches for the Bar, and a table for each jury room, and benches for the same are to be finished; the three inside doors to be temporary; a seat and writing table for Clerk, to be made between the bench and the Bar. Note—The house to be raised, shingled, weather boarded and floored, and the bench for the Judge and Justices, Judge or Chairman's writing desk, Clerk's seat and table, the bar and table and benches therefor, the four windows below and two above to be finished, the rest of the windows cased and nailed up. The front door to be finished, and the other three temporary doors to be made and hung. Comprehends the present contract proposed by the Court to be performed by the next Assizes for this District.

DECEMBER the 10th, 1803.—The contract was let to Job Lodor for 250 pounds.

MAY 19th, 1804.—The site of the Gaol seems to have again engaged the attention of the Justices, after making an examination of it they gave as their opinion that the "Debtor's room is sufficient for the reception of prisoners of that description excepting the lock, which the Court agrees to send for." An agreement was also made with Mr. Job Lodor to undertake the business of Gaoler for the salary of £25 which the Court agreed to allow him for one year.

DECEMBER 11th, 1804.—The Court of Quarter Sessions Assembled at the Court House, but immediately adjourned to the house of Job Lodor.

JANUARY 26th, 1805.-We have an evidence of settlement in the Township of Dunwich, the Court ordering "that the Township of Dunwich be included in the next year's assessment with that of Delaware."

MARCH 12th, 1805.—Application was made by Thomas Noland, "to be recomended for the purpose of obtaining a license to keep a house of public entertainment at Port Talbot in the Township of Dunwich. Allowed."

MARCH 13th, 1805.—The following amusing case is reported : John McColl is brought into Court in custody of the under Sheriff, charged with high crimes and misdemeanors by William Hutchison, Esquire. John McColl, the prisoner, asked William Hutchison, Esquire, "What he wanted with him?" William Hutchison, Esquire, in answer said, "To find Bail for the Peace and good behaviour and your appearance at the next Assizes."

The prisoner said: "Will you take land, or horses, or money, or dogs for the security, I have two good dogs." William Hutchison Esquire, answering said : "No, none but personal security will do."

Benajah Mallory, Esquire, appearing at the Bar, William Hutchison, Esquire, threatened to send him to gaol, and demanded bail for his good behaviour, which Benajah Mallory positively refused to give, said he had done nothing and plead priviledge, as being a member of Parliament.

The prisoner John McColl, said : "Speak up Captain Mallory, you are a gentleman, you are the only gentleman in the house," William Hutchison, Esquire, said : "If you open your mouth again,

I will order you to be put in the stocks. "The prisoner then gaped his mouth wide open and said: "I shall want some more whiskey." William Hutchison, Esquire, then ordered the prisoner to be put in the stocks, and the under Sheriff commanding assistance took the prisoner out of the Court room and reported upon oath with the oath also of the High Constable that the prisoner was rescued out of their hands by Philip Fonger, Constable of Charlotteville, Joseph Miller, of Charlotteville, Miller; Peter Coombs, of Charlotteville, Carpenter; Robert Munro, of Charlotteville, Farmer; and many others, and by the oath of Henry Bostwick and the under Sheriff, that Anthony Sells of Charlotteville laborer, being commanded to assist in putting the prisoner in the stocks, disobeyed those orders and fled.

13th JUNE, 1805.—In order to better maintain the dignity of Court, it was decided to procure 12 staves for the Constables of the District, the staves to be seven feet in length and one and three-quarter inches in thickness with the name of the Township on each staff in plain legible letters.

NOVEMBER 16th, 1805.—A Commission was received appointing John Bostwick, Sheriff of the District of London.

11th DECEMBER 1805.—That the Whipping Post previously erected was used, is shown by the record of the case of The King vs. Peter Coombs, indicted of petty larceny, on this date. "The sentence of the Court upon the prisoner is that he shall receive 20 lashes on his bare back, well laid on, the Sheriff being ordered by the Court to have the above sentence put into immediate execution." It is done accordingly.

That the prisoners in the District Gaol were not allowed to have a fire in the building is shewn by the record of the Petition of Ebenezer Allan, presented to the Court on this date, when it was ordered that Ebenezer Allen, the prisoner above named be allowed the use of fire in the Gaol provided he, the said prisoner, secured the Sheriff to his satisfaction, and if the Sheriff is willing to comply with this additional order, and not otherwise.

MARCH 12th, 1806.—The system of paying members of the Provincial Legislature at this time was different from that of the present day. The following entry appears on this date, "It is ordered that a full rate of assessment be collected for the present year, and one-fifth be added to pay Benajah Mallory Esquire, the representative in Parliament in this District for his services as such, for 39 days in the second session of the fourth Provincial Parliament at 10 Shillings per day amounting to 19 pounds 10 shillings."

JUNE 10th, 1806.—Thomas Talbot's name appears for the first time among those of the Justices in Session, and he attended for one day only. During the next few years there is nothing to shew that he took any interest whatever in the proceedings of these Courts.

JUNE 10th, 1807.—Ebenezer Green was appointed Constable for Dunwich and Aldborough, and Thomas Talbot, James Burdick, Archibald McMillan, and Daniel Springer were appointed Members of the Court of Request for the County of Middlesex. The Legislature having granted money to the District for the purpose of Roads, it was agreed that 50 pounds be expended in the Township of Westminster, and 150 pounds on the north side of the River Thames, so as to meet the provincial road through the Western District, and the members of the Court of Request, with the exception of Colonel Talbot, were appointed to superintend the surveying and laying out of the road.

The increased dignity and importance of the Quarter Sessions Court is shewn by the following order: "That no person whatever shall be admitted within the Bar unless business calls him there, and that a Constable do attend at the entrance of the door to stop any person coming in who has no business there, except asked in by the Court."

SEPTEMBER 9th, 1807.—The financial business of the District having assumed sufficient proportions, it was ordered "that a book should be purchased for the purpose of entering all accounts which shall pass this Court in future, and that all former accounts as far as the same shall be ascertained, shall be entered in the said book particularly specifying the particulars of each respective account."

DECEMBER 8th, 1807.—The Grand Jury declare themselves entirely satisfied with the Treasurer's account up to the year

1806 inclusive, and said that in this account a wolfs' scalp which was in arrears was accounted for.

That there was a difficulty in making collection of taxes levied by the District Court, is shown by a reference in nearly every session to the dilatory manner in which the Collectors made their returns.

In 1808 John Quick was appointed Constable for Dunwich, and Samuel Guarnsay was appointed Collector.

JUNE 14th, 1809.—Joseph Smith was appointed Constable for Dunwich.

TURKEY POINT.

TURKEY POINT, was an original Government Reservation selected by Governor Simcoe, for a Town and Garrison.

In 1798, instructions were issued by D. W. Smith, A.S.G., to Mr. Welch, "to take a sketch of the ground above the point which may be suitable for a town. The ground immediately above Mrs. Mabee's old house has been set apart and approved for that purpose. * * * In the projection of this sketch you will have regard to such a situation as may be fit for Barracks and such other accomodation as may be looked for in providing space for a small fort." It was situated in the South-West part of the Township of Charlotteville, and was at one time called "Port Norfolk."

THE LONDON DISTRICT.

Dr. Ryerson, in "The Loyalist of America," published a historical memoranda by Mrs. Amelia Harris, of Eldon House, London, Ontario, only daughter of the late Colonel Samuel Ryerse who settled at Long Point, (Port Ryerson) in 1794. She refers to the formation of the London District as follows :

"About this time the London District was separated from the Western, and composed what now forms the Counties or District of Middlesex, Elgin, Huron Bruce, Oxford and Norfolk. The necessary appointments were made, and the London District held its own courts and sessions at Turkey Point, six miles above us on the Lake Shore. The people, in a most patriotic manner, had put up a log house, which served the double purpose of court house and gaol. The Courts were held in the upper story, which was entered by a very rough stairway, going upon the outside of the building. The gaol consisted of one large room on the ground floor, from which any prisoner could release himself in half an hour unless guarded by a sentinel. The juries for some years held their consultations under the shade of a tree. Doubtless it was pleasanter than the close lock-up jury-room of the present day. My father, in addition to his other commissions, was appointed Judge of District Court and Judge of the Surrogate Court. Turkey Point is a very pretty place; the grounds are high, and from them there is a very fine view of the bay and lake.

2. General Simcoe had selected it for a County Town, and the site of a future city. Now it boasts of one house, an inn kept by Silas Montross. There was also a reservation of land for Military purposes. But the town never prospered; it was not in a thoroughfare, and did not possess water privileges.

Twenty years afterwards it contained but the one solitary house. The County town was changed to a more favorable situation, Vittoria."

COURTS.

From 1800 to 1803 the Courts were held in the house of Mr. James Munro, in the Township of Charlotteville. In the latter year they were moved to the house of Mr. Job Lodor, innkeeper, situated at Turkey Point, he having furnished increased accommodations, and were continued to be holden there until a log gaol and a two story framed Court House were erected near the same place, at the expense of the district by Mr. Job Lodor, the contractor. In this Court House the Courts were held in the first story, and the second was divided off for Jury rooms.

The Courts continued to be held at this house until it became necessary to appropriate the building for the use of the Troops, during the war of 1812,—'13 and '14. (From the Oxford *Gazetteer* by Thos. S. Shenston.)

RECORDS.

The Records of the Quarter Sessions Courts with the exception of the years 1810,—11,—12, are complete.

Early reports of the Assize Courts are very irregular, and, with few exceptions, are of little use for historical purposes.

The names of the Judges who attended these Courts were Powell, Allcock, Scott and Thorpe. They always came by water and were often several days behind time in consequence of the weather.

The first entry in the Road Register of the London District was made by J. B. Askin, Clerk of the Peace, under an order of Session dated 12th January, 1822. The entry shews an examination by A. A. Rapelje, Surveyor for the Townships of Walpole and Rainham, of a road from the bank of Lake Erie, on the eastern line of Rainham Township to the western limits of the Township of Walpole. Richard Bristol, deputy surveyor, laid out a road January 11th, 1821, from the line between lots five and six Talbot Street to the conflux of Otter Creek and Lake Erie. In 1821, Louis Burwell Deputy for John Bostwick, surveyor, laid out a road from the mouth of Kettle Creek to Talbot road. In 1822 part of this road from Goodhue's mills to their still house, was reported unpracticable and the road was altered so as to run from the mill by the house of Daniel Rapelje, and thence to the summit of the said hill, keeping along the brow on the lands of William Drake.

Note—This is the road leading from Turvill's Mills, in St. Thomas, north around the bend of the hill west of the Court House.

COURT OF REQUESTS.

The Court of Requests established by 32 Geo., III Chap. 6, provided for the trial by two or more Justices of the Peace of all disputes in the matter of debt and contract where the amount involved did not exceed ten pounds.

VITTORIA.

In 1815 an Act was passed to repeal Sec. of 41 Geo. III, Chap. 6, which provided that the Courts of General Quarter Sessions for the District of London should be holden at Charlotteville, and providing that from and after the passing of the Act "the Courts of the General Quarter Sessions of the Peace and the District

Courts in and for the said District shall be holden and assemble at the most convenient place in the immediate vicinity of Tisdale's Mills in the Township of Charlotteville in the said District, and the Magistrates at the next ensuing Quarter Sessions of the Peace to be holden in and for the said District, shall be and they are hereby authorized to make choice of a place in the vicinity of the said Mills in the Township of Charlotteville as aforesaid whereon to erect a Gaol and Court House for the said District." The Magistrates as directed, decided to erect a gaol and Court House for the said District at Vittoria, which is situated near the eastern corner of the Township of Charlotteville, and it was here that a brick Court House was built, at an expense of Nine Thousand Pounds; the Government contributing Two Thousand Pounds. This building was used until 1826 when it was partially destroyed by fire.

To describe the proceedings of the Courts held at Vittoria the following extracts are taken from the Pioneer Sketches by Garrett Oakes, Esquire, who speaks from personal observation having attended as Constable and Juryman. "All Magistrates and Constables were in those days ordered to attend at each session of the Court of King's Bench or pay a penalty, for at these Courts the Grand Juries were composed of Magistrates only, and as there were four Quarter Sessions annually the Constables were in duty bound to attend five Courts each year. As I was living fifty miles from Vittoria I had to travel going and returning three hundred miles a year, or nine hundred miles in three years. This I had to do on foot, at the same time carrying provisions to last until my return home, and I had to do it without one cent to pay. There was no accommodation at Vittoria for one-tenth of those attending Court. But I had plenty of company every night when there. We used to make field beds in the Court Room with our knapsacks of provisions as a substitute for pillows. During our absence from home we were usually unable to get a cup of tea or coffee to assist deglutition. But the Jurymen had the advantage of the Constable, for when a case of debt was tried each juror received twenty cents from the prosecutor. Yet those of us who lived within fifty miles of Vittoria were favored, when compared with such as lived at the western limit of Middlesex, for these had to travel one hundred miles to attend Court when their only road was made by clearing off the underwood and old logs to the width of twelve or fifteen feet, a road that went winding between and around big trees, and following the high ground to avoid the swamps and impassable places. It was inevitably necessary to sleep two nights in the woods before reaching Vittoria, and the same of course on the return journey."

LONDON.

In 1826 an Act was passed to " establish a District Town in the District of London in a more central position than at present," and enacted "that the Courts of General Quarter Sessions of the Peace and the District Courts should be holden and assembled in some part of the reservation heretofore made for the site of a town near the forks of the River Thames in the Townships of London and Westminster in the County of Middlesex. General Simcoe, afterwards Governor, when making a tour through Upper Canada, gave as his opinion that the forks of the Thames would be an eligible situation for a town. This site was surveyed by Colonel M. Burwell in 1826 under the authority of an Act passed in that year which ordered "that the Town shall be surveyed and laid out under the direction of the Surveyor General within the Reservation heretofore made for the site of a town in the Townships of London and Westminster in the County of Middlesex in the said District of London." The Act directed that a tract or space of land not less than four acres should be designated as reserved for the purpose of Gaol and Court House within the said Town plot. Thomas Talbot, Mahlon Burwell James Hamilton, Charles Ingersoll and John Matthews were appointed Commissioners for the purpose of erecting on said reserved tract as aforesaid, a good and sufficient Gaol and Court House of brick or stone, and for the purposes of defraying the expenses of erection of the building, the Commissioners were authorized to raise by way of loan, the sum of Four Thousand Pounds, and to levy an additional rate of one third of a penny on the pound until this sum and all interest thereon were paid. The Commissioners were ordered to hold their first meeting in St. Thomas. Garrett Oakes, in his pioneer, sketches refers to the location of the Court House at London as follows:—" When the Court House at Vittoria was burned it was determined to erect a new one on a' reserve made by Governor Simcoe, the first Governor of Upper Canada, for the site of a town to be called London. The building was constructed of flat logs, and on the ground floor was a log partition to separate the gaol from the gaoler's room. The Court room above was reached by stairs outside. As soon as the house was roofed, William Parke, the old Vittoria Gaoler, removed to London to assume his office in the new building, and I assisted him to finish the Court room in a rough manner as a makeshift until the new Court house should be ready for occupation. In the year 1828 I attended Court in London."

Up to the year 1834 the Justices in Session managed all local matters pretty much as they pleased, and in that year an Act was passed which provided that the inhabitant householders at their annual township meetings should appoint not less than three nor more than eighteen persons to be fence viewers. The meetings were also authorized to determine what should be considered a lawful fence, and the Act provided at great length what the powers, duties and remuneration of fence viewers should be, and how their decisions should be enforced. By this Act also provision was made for opening ditches and watercourses among the several persons interested, as the fence viewers might decide.

In 1835 an important change was made; several Acts previously passed respecting town meetings were repealed, and it was provided that the Township Clerk should assemble the inhabitants of the Township being house holders and free holders at a place agreed upon at the previous yearly meeting. This meeting was empowered to choose the following Township officers:—The Clerk, three Commissioners, one Assessor, one Collector, and any number of persons they thought proper to serve as overseers of Highways, Roads and Bridges and as Pound Keepers. The Collectors gave bonds to the District Treasurer to whom they paid the proceeds of the rates levied, and the Township Clerks gave bonds to the Commissioners. The most important change was the appointment of Commissioners to whom were now transferred many of the powers respecting the construction and repairs of bridges and roads previously held and exercised by the Justices in Quarter Sessions. The Board of Commissioners were required to meet three times at the place in which the last Township meeting was held, and were authorized to hold as many other meetings as they thought best at any place they choose. They were to receive from the District Treasurer Five Shillings per day for their services. The Quarter Sessions still maintained the authority they formerly held in reference to the administration of Justice, the location and alteration of highways and other matters general to the District. This was the Municipal system in vogue at the time of the Rebellion of 1837, which led to the abolition of separate Provincial Governments and brought about Legislative union.

DISTRICT OF LONDON OR COUNTY OF MIDDLESEX—1837 to 1852.

In March 1837, an Act was passed setting apart the County of Oxford as the District of Brock and the County of Norfolk as the District of Talbot, so that we have now to consider only the County of Middlesex or District of London.

Up to this time no mention has been made of the Townships of Malahide and Bayham. When the Counties of Norfolk, Oxford and Middlesex were formed in 1798 these Townships had not been surveyed, but were unoccupied territory, included within the boundaries of the District of London. When surveyed in 1810 by M. Burwell, they were not placed in any particular County. In 1837, when the Counties of Oxford and Norfolk were set apart as the Districts of Brock and Talbot respectively, Norfolk included only the Townships referred to in the Act of 1798, leaving these Townships in the County of Middlesex.

In 1839, the Township Commissioners provided for in the Act of 1835, were named Town Wardens. The change whereby the people were intrusted with the freest of action in the election of municipal officers, viz: the Clerk, Assessor, Collector, Commissioners or Wardens does not seem to have been much in the direction of popular self-government, as officers thus chosen were not intrusted with any of the duties or powers which are necessary for really efficient Municipal Government, but any Act that took from the nominative Magistracy any of the powers they exercised was appreciated. This system was continued up to the year 1841, when the legislature of the United Provinces endeavored to create a municipal system that would meet all the requirements of Upper Canada.

In 1840 the authorities recognized the necessity of leaving the people free to control their own internal affairs and giving up that system of paternal government which had worked so unsatisfactorily. Some difficulties arose in dealing with this question on account of the position taken by Lower Canada. During the suspension of the constitution in French Canada an ordinance had been passed by a special Council to provide for the better internal government of the Province for the establishment of local or municipal institutions therein.

The Province was divided into Districts and the Governor and Council determined the number of Councillors and appointed the Warden. Consequently the system in operation in Lower Canada was entirely controlled by the Government. It was the desire of the Upper Canadians, who had been gradually educated for more popular local institutions, to elect the Warden and their officers. This furnished the basis of the Municipal Act of 1841 which provided for District Councils, to be composed of one or two members to be elected at the regular meeting in each Township, and hold office for three years, retiring in rotation; the Council was required to meet four times a year. The Warden, Treasurer and Clerk were appointed by the Governor of the Province. Every By-Law passed had to be approved of by the Provincial authorities. The Governor had the power to dissolve District Councils at any time. To the District Councils were transferred the powers of the Quarter Sessions with reference to the administration of municipal affairs.

On the 10th February, 1842, the first District Council in the County of Middlesex met at London. Andrew Moore and John Burwell represented Bayham; Daniel Able and James Brown, Malahide; Thomas Hutchinson and John Oill, Yarmouth; George Elliott and Levi Fowler, Southwold; Thomas Coyne, Dunwich; Thomas Duncan, Aldborough; William Niles, Dorchester. John Wilson was appointed Warden by the Governor and George S. Fraser, Clerk *pro tem.*, and the appointment of Mr. J. B. Strathey as Clerk of the District Council was announced before the second meeting in May of the same year. The Council of the London District continued until 1849, when a municipal system essentially the same as that we enjoy to-day was introduced. The inhabitants of every Township having one hundred or more resident free-holders or house-holders on the tax collectors' Roll were made a body corporate. The Township Council was to consist of five members elected by a general Township vote or by Wards. The Councillors were to elect one of themselves Reeve and a Deputy Reeve for each 500 freeholders or householders on the Collectors' List. Townships containing less than one hundred free holders and householders were by By-Law of the District Councils to be attached to some other adjacent township. Under the present system the Reeve is elected by the direct vote of the electors as are also the Deputy Reeves in Townships not divided into Wards. In Townships divided into Wards, a Reeve and four Councillors are elected, and the Councillors appoint from among themselves a Deputy Reeve for each 500 names on the Township Voters' List.

COUNTY OF ELGIN.

In July of the year 1846 an agitation for the partition of the extensive district of Middlesex was commenced. The principal reasons urged were that it was two unwield to manage its own affairs with prudence and economy, that the inhabitants of the Townships east and west of St. Thomas had to pass through that place on their way to London, that the interests of the northern and southern portions of the district were separate, that no improvements of importance had been made in the southern part of the District, that everything was done to benefit London and its immediate neighhorhood. The principal objection urged was the expense of building a Court House and Gaol. In the month of August official notice was given that an application would be made to the Provincial Parliament at its next session, for setting off the Townships of Aldborough, Dunwich, Southwold, Yarmouth, Malahide, Bayham and South Dorchester into a new District. On the morning of Thursday, the 27th day of August the Town of St. Thomas put on its gayest appearance. The St. George's Amateur Band made a circuit of the Township passing through the villages of Sparta and New Sarum, and returning to St. Thomas at 12 o'clock noon, the hour appointed for a general meeting of the inhabitants to take into consideration the most feasible means of obtaining a partition of the London District. The balcony of the Mansion House in which the meeting was held wore a splendid appearance. Flags were flying ; a diagram of the old District, and banners inscribed "Our Queen and Country, a Division of the District" presented by Mr. Walthew assisted in improving the appearance of this important meeting. Murdock McKenzie Esquire, was appointed to the Chair, and T. Hodge, Esquire, Secretary. Resolutions were passed unanimously and with unbounded applause approving of the proposition presented for the separation of the District, and it was in this way that the first impetus was given to the movement which resulted in St. Thomas being made the County Town of the new District. As an inducement Mr. Benjamin Drake offered gratuitously a sufficient quantity of land in the most central part of the Town for a site for a Market place, Court House and Gaol. A large Executive Committee having been appointed, meetings were ordered to be held to take the sense of the other Townships. The "Canadian Freeman" published in St. Thomas, advocated very strongly the division of the District, and the "Western Globe" published in London, expressed the views and opinions of the opposition.

Among the Villages in the County which were at this time in a flourishing condition, are mentioned : Hall's Mills, Yarmouth Mills, Talbot Mills, Jamestown and St. George's Town ; of these but very little trace can be found at the present time.

Among the different propositions for the division of the District that were prominently advocated, was that Malahide, Bayham and South Dorchester, Houghton, Middleton and part of Durham should form a separate District with Vienna as the County Town. Considerable opposition emanated from Port Stanley, where the people were at first warm advocates for division, but when it was ascertained that St. Thomas and not Port Stanley, would likely be the County Town of the new District, they got up an opposition Petition.

The Legislature seems to have been considering a general Act for the Division of the Counties and Districts of the Province, and the matter was delayed during some two sessions. In 1851

L. Burwell, Chairman of a Committee of the London District Council, appointed to consider a proposal for the division of the County reported as follows :—" Understanding that the Government intend, during the ensuing session, to introduce a Bill for the purpose of dividing the larger Counties, your Committee have given attention to that portion referring to Middlesex. Your Committee are of the opinion that the division line proposed, running east and west, embracing the six frontier townships, and portions of Delaware, Westminster and Dorchester, will be opposed by a majority of the inhabitants of this County, and that a division for other than electoral purposes is unnecessary; and that for electoral purposes the line should run north and south, embracing Dunwich, Aldborough, Mosa, Ekfrid, Caradoc, Metcalfe, Lobo, Adelaide and Williams, as the new County, and that the same be called the County of Elgin." This Committee further reported in favor of giving Bayham to Oxford County in *lieu* of a portion of Nissouri to be attached to Middlesex.

In August of the same year an Act was passed establishing the County of Elgin to consist of seven Townships as at present. The Counties of Middlesex and Elgin were to be united for Municipal, Judicial and other purposes. This Act also provided for the division of the Township of Dorchester at the line between the 6th and 7th concessions south of the River Thames. The Act made provision, by Proclamation of the Governor, for the Town Reeves and Deputy Reeves of certain Counties including Elgin, to be formed into provisional municipal Councils, and also provided for the dissolution of the union of the Counties so soon as the Court House and Gaol was erected and completed at the County Town.

Under the authority of a proclamation bearing the signature and Seal of James Hamilton, Sheriff, Upper Canada, Middlesex and Elgin, the provisional Council of the County of Elgin met in the Town Hall, St. Thomas, at 12 o'clock noon on the 15th April, 1852; David Parish was Chairman appointed by proclamation. The following were members of the Provisional Council :—

Duncan McColl,	Reeve,	Aldborough.
Moses Willey,	Reeve,	Dunwich.
Colin Munro,	Reeve,	Southwold.

Nicol McColl,	Deputy Reeve,	Southwold.
Elisha S. Ganson,	Reeve,	Yarmouth.
Leslie Pierce,	Deputy Reeve,	Yarmouth.
David Parish,	Reeve,	St. Thomas.
Thomas Locker,	Reeve,	Malahide.
Lewis J. Clarke,	Deputy Reeve,	Malahide.
Jacob Cline,	Reeve,	South Dorchester.
John Elliott,	Reeve,	Bayham.
J. Skinner,	Deputy Reeve,	Bayham.

E. S. Ganson, was elected Warden.

The erection of the County buildings was then proceeded with on a block of land donated to the County of Elgin by Benjamin Drake, Esquire, and in September 1853, an agreement was arrived at by the Committees appointed by the two Counties to adjust the debt between them preparatory to dissolution.

In accordance with the Proclamation dissolving the union of the united Counties of Middlesex and Elgin published in the Canada Gazette, the 30th day of September, 1853, the first meeting of the County Council of the County of Elgin was held in County Buildings, St. Thomas, on Tuesday, the 8th day of November 1853. Thomas Locker, was Warden at this time.

Ontario Historical Society
1900.
TORONTO.

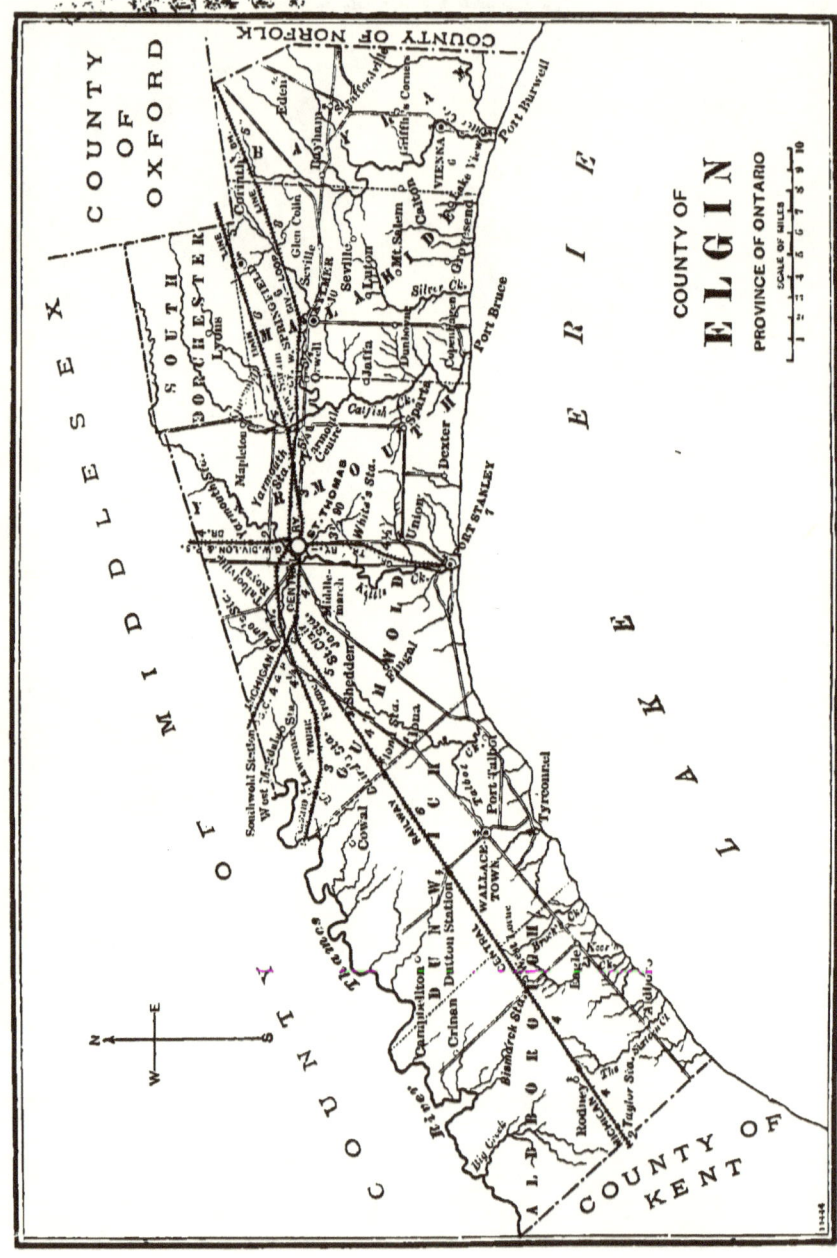

Ontario Historical Society
1900
TORONTO.

SURVEYS.

Statement of the several Townships comprised in the County of Middlesex before its Division, with the dates of survey, superficial extent in acres of each Township, and names of the surveyors by whom the surveys were made.

TOWNSHIP.	DATE OF SURVEY.	SUPERFICIAL ACRES.	NAME OF SURVEYOR.	REMARKS.
Aldborough	1797		Law & Hambly	1, 2, and 3 Con., Law, West Line, Hambly.
Aldborough	1803		Hambly	
Aldborough	1797	78,000	Law	Crown & Clergy Res.
A. and Dunwich	1811		M. Burwell	Talbot Road.
Aldborough	1832		Carroll	
Dunwich	1799		Hambly	Line between S. & D.
Dunwich	1803		Hambly	5 to 12 Con., E. Line.
Dunwich	1832	70,000	Springer	Con. A. B., 1 to 11 & S. W. & N. E. Boundar's
Dun. and Aldborough	1811		M. Burwell	Talbot Road through—see Aldborough.
Dunwich			Lowe	1, 2, 3, and 4th Cons.
Southwold	1819		M. Burwell	South part.
Southwold	1830		M. Burwell	North part.
Southwold	1797		Hambly	R. Thames in Southw'd
Southwold	1797		Hambly	Traverse of the front and part of outlines.
Southwold	1809	68,600	M. Burwell	also Yarmouth etc
Southwold	1809		M. Burwell	Talbot Road through.
Southwold	1850		C. Fraser	Part of 3rd Con. under 12 Vic. C. 35, Sec. 31.
Southwold	1854		C. Fraser	Municipal survey of Talbot road E and W.
Yarmouth	1799		Jones	
Yarmouth	1809	71,000	M. Burwell	See Southwold.
Yarmouth	1819		M. Burwell	
Malahide	1809		M. Burwell	Talbot road through.
Malahide	1810	59,400	M. Burwell	
Bayham	1818		M. Burwell	
Bayham	1809	60,000	M. Burwell	Talbot road through.
Dorchester S	1810		Wilmot (partial.)	E. & W. & base line 1, 2, 3, 4, 5, 6, 7, 8, 9, 10, 11, 12, & 13 Con.
Dorchester North	1799	32,600 N 43,200 S	Hambly	1, 2, 3, 4, and 5th Con and Western line.
Dorchester North	1799		Hambly	River Thames in
Dorchester S			Lowe	1, 2 and 3 Concessions
Dorchester S	1793		Jones	
Dorchester S	1847		Wm. Smiley	Clergy lots Cons A & B.
D. and Westminster	1852		C. Fraser	Line between (survey under 12 Vic. C. 35)
Dorchester North	1858		Wm. McMillan	Municipal survey line between 1st and 2nd cons S. of Thames.
Dorchester North	1858		S. Peters	Municipal survey E. Survey of 1st Con. line (S. D.)

TOWNSHIP.	DATE OF SURVEY.	SUPERFICIAL ACRES.	NAME OF SURVEYOR.	REMARKS.
Dorchester North	1859		S. Peters	Municipal survey Con. B (S. D.)
Dorchester North	1859		W. G. Wonham	Municipal survey by line between N. D. & N. Oxford.
Westminster	1820		Burwell	Partial connecting Talbot Road
Westminster	1824		Burwell	and London Wharncliffe Highway.
Westminster	1821		Mount	2nd Concession.
Westminster	1810		Watson	Traverse of Thames & 1, 2, and 3 Cons.
Westminster		36,600	Bostwick	3rd to 9th Cons.
W. and Dorchester	1852		C. Fraser	See Dorchester. Line between (survey under 12V. C. 35.)
Westminster	1839		P. Carroll for Bound'y Comr's.	Part of B. and 1 Con.
Westminster	1857		C. Fraser	Municipal Survey 2nd Concession
Westminster	1859		Wm. McMillan	Municipal Survey line in front of 2 Con
London (town)	1836		Carroll	
London (town)	1810		Burwell	1st to 5th Con. (see Westminster).
London (town)	1819		Burwell	6th to 16th Cons. A. B. and C. Cons.
London (town)	1833		Rankin	Mill privilege
London Road	1830		McDonald	2nd & 3rd Con. E & W of London Road.
London	1829		McDonald	Front tier of lots.
London Townplot	1825		M. Burwell	
London Millsite	1846		Carroll	
London Township	1855	105,200	B. Springer	Lots 31, 32, 11th Con. (Municipal S)
Lobo	1820		Burwell	Part of W. line B F. & 1st & 2nd Con. and line between 10 and 11 lots
Lobo	1820	48,600	Burwell	W. line 3 to 13 Con. and side roads also rear line.
Delaware	1798		Hambly	2, 3, 4, & 5th Con. & S. Boundary.
Delaware	1793	27,600	Jones	1 & 2 Cons. and river lots.
Delaware	1852		W. McMillan	Survey under 12th Vic. C. 35 1st Con.
Delaware	1855		B. Springer	Municipal Survey lots 31 & 32 11th Con.
Ekfrid	1820	56,150	Burwell	2nd to 8th Con. E. & W. and rear lines.
Ekfrid	1820		Burwell	Long woods road and ranges in rear.
Mosa	1820	49,600	Burwell	
Adelaide	1833		Carroll	
Adelaide Village	1833	43,000	Carroll	

The above is a list certified by the Assistant Commissioner, Crown Lands Department, Quebec, 5th March, 1860.

NOTE:—There is however in the Crown Lands Department a map by Augustus Jones, the Surveyor, of his survey of the North-west part of Southwold, made in the year 1794. It shows the base-line and the Concessions running from it to the Dunwich town line. The field notes of this survey were never fyled, and were no doubt lost or destroyed.

* * * *

Patents for lots in Dunwich were issued in 1795. So that an early survey in that Township was overlooked by the Crown Lands Department in making up the above statements.

* * * *

The original instructions under which the Townships were named and blocked out before being sub-divided into lots have not been found.

* * * *

By 16 Vic., Chap. 225, Errors in the early surveys of Aldborough were corrected.

PARLIAMENTARY REPRESENTATIVES.

UPPER CANADA LEGISLATURE 1792 TO 1841.

Year of Election.	(Norfolk and 4th Riding of Lincoln)	Suffolk and Essex.
1792	D. W. Smith.	James Baby.
1797	D. W. Smith.	James Baby.

	London District.
1800	D. W. Smith.
1804	Benajah Mallory
1809	Benajah Mallory

	Norfolk	Oxford and Middlesex
1813	Robert Nicol.	M. Burwell.
1817	Robert Nicol.	M. Burwell.

During the fifth Session of the Seventh Parliament, (March, 1820) an act was passed which provided "that from and after "the end of the present Parliament each and every County now "formed or organized or that may hereafter be organized the "population of which shall amount to one thousand souls, shall "be represented by one member and such County or Counties "that amount to four thousand souls by two members." Mr. Burwell in his address to the electors of the County of Middlesex at the next general election says: "By the provisions of "this law of which I had the honor of being the mover a "County having a population of one thousand souls will return "one member to the House and a County having a population of "four thousand souls will return two members, so that the "County of Oxford with which we have heretofore been incor- "porated will this Session send its own member and the County "of Middlesex one." *Oxford Gazetteer by T. S. Shenston.*

COUNTY OF MIDDLESEX.

1820	Mahlon Burwell.	
1825	John Matthews.	John Rolph.
1829	John Matthews.	John Rolph.
1831	Mahlon Burwell.	Roswell Mount.
1835	Elias Moore.	Thomas Park.
1836	Elias Moore.	Thomas Park.

UNITED PARLIAMENT 1841 TO 1867.

COUNTY OF MIDDLESEX.

1841	Thomas Park.
1844	Edward Ermatinger.
1848	William Notman.

MIDDLESEX AND ELGIN.

1852	Crowell Wilson.

COUNTY OF ELGIN.

	East Riding.	West Riding.
1854	George Southwick.	George Macbeth.
1857	Leonidas Burwell.	George Macbeth.
1861	Leonidas Burwell.	George Macbeth. (‡)
1863	Leonidas Burwell.	John Scoble.

(‡) On petition Mr. Macbeth was unseated and Mr. Scoble took his place,

ONTARIO LEGISLATURE 1867 TO 1895.

1867	D. Luton.	Nicol McColl.
1871	J. H. Wilson.	Thomas Hodgins.
1875	J. H. Wilson.	Malcolm G. Munro. (*)
1878		David McLaws.
1879	T. M. Nairn. (ob.)	John Cascaden.
1883	C. O. Ermatinger.	John Cascaden.
1886	T. M. Nairn.	A. B. Ingram.
1888	J. C. Dance.	
1890	H. T. Godwin.	Dugald McColl.
1894	C. A. Brower.	Donald Macnish.

HOUSE OF COMMONS 1867 TO 1895.

	West Elgin	East Elgin
1867	John H. Munro.	T. W. Dobbie.
1872	George E. Casey.	Wm. Harvey.
1874	George E. Casey.	Wm. Harvey. (ob.)
1874		Colin Macdougall.
1878	George E. Casey.	Thomas Arkell.
1882	George E. Casey.	John H Wilson.
1887	George E. Casey.	John H. Wilson.
1891	George E. Casey.	A. B. Ingram.

(*) Mr. Munro was unseated by the Court and Mr. Hodgins sat from 1875 to 1878, when he resigned in order to become a candidate in Toronto for the House of Commons.

LIST OF WARDENS COUNTY OF ELGIN.

Year	Name	Municipality
1852	E. S. GANSON AND THOMAS LOCKER	Provisional Wardens
1853	THOMAS LOCKER	Malahide
1854	THOMAS LOCKER	Malahide
1855	THOMAS LOCKER	Malahide
1856	RANDOLPH JOHNSON	Yarmouth
1857	RANDOLPH JOHNSON	Yarmouth
1858	LEVI FOWLER	Southwold
1859	LEVI FOWLER	Southwold
1860	JAMES ARMSTRONG	Yarmouth
1861	J. H. JONES	Bayham
1862	J. H. JONES	Bayham
1863	DANIEL LUTON	Yarmouth
1864	GEORGE SUFFEL	Vienna
1865	JOHN CLUNAS	Dorchester
1866	T. M. NAIRN	Malahide
1867	T. M. NAIRN	Malahide
1868	T. M. NAIRN	Malahide
1869	T. M. NAIRN	Malahide
1870	T. M. NAIRN	Malahide
1871	T. M. NAIRN	Malahide
1872	JOHN ELLISON	Southwold
1873	JOHN MCCAUSLAND	Malahide
1874	JOHN MCCAUSLAND	Malahide
1875	GEORGE SUFFEL	Vienna
1876	GEORGE SUFFEL	Vienna
1877	SAMUEL DAY	Yarmouth
1878	EDWARD HEGLER	Dorchester
1879	T. W. KIRKPATRICK	Aldborough
1880	JAMES MARTIN	Yarmouth
1881	MANUEL PAYNE	Port Stanley
1882	J. B. MILLS	Springfield
1883	JOHN A. MILLER	Yarmouth
1884	A. J. LEITCH	Dunwich
1885	SAMUEL S. CLUTTON	Aylmer
1886	JAMES HEPBURN	Yarmouth
1887	J. C. DANCE	S. Dorchester
1888	DONALD TURNER	Southwold
1889	H. T. GODWIN	Bayham
1890	JOHN J. STALKER	Aldborough
1891	A. N. CLINE	S. Dorchester
1892	M. E. LYON	Malahide
1893	A. A. MCKILLOP	Dunwich
1894	W. M. FORD	Bayham
1895	JOHN THOMPSON	Aldborough

MUNICIPAL NOMENCLATURE.

The County was named Elgin in honor of the Earl of Elgin, Governor-General of Canada from 1847 to 1854.

TOWNSHIPS.

Aldborough so called after a Town in the County of Suffolk England. The township was in the County of Suffolk when surveyed in 1797.

Dunwich so called for the same reasons as those given in the case of Aldborough and also as a compliment to Earl Stradbroke, who was called Viscount Dunwich and whose family name was Rous.

Southwold was called after a Seaport in Suffolk, England, for the same reasons as those given in the case of Aldborough.

Yarmouth was so called after a seaport town in the County of Norfolk near the boundary of Suffolk and also as a compliment to Francis Seymour or Lord Cornway, who in 1793 was made Earl of Yarmouth.

Malahide owes the origin of its name to Malahide Castle, the home of Richard Talbot, father of Colonel Talbot.

Bayham was so called as a compliment to Lord Camden, who was Viscount Bayham. Lord Camden was Secretary-of-war and Colonies in 1804 and Lord President of the Council 1805-7.

TOWNS.

Dutton was named after an official employed in the construction of the Canada Southern Railway.

Aylmer was first called Troy, but in 1835, just before the Rebellion, a meeting was held in Caswell's wagon shop to decide upon a name for the place. The majority were in favor of Troy, but the name Aylmer, from Lord Aylmer, then Governor-General, was in some manner sent to the Post Office Department.

St. Thomas was named as a compliment to Thomas Talbot, the founder of the settlement.

Springfield so called when the grist mill in the east end of the village was raised over a large spring, one of many in the village. The post office, "Clunas," was afterwards moved one mile south and the name changed to to Springfield.

Vienna was first named Shrewsberry by Col. Burwell, but the people did not like the name, so it was named Vienna by the Edison family, who were quite influential people, their ancestors having originally come from Vienna, Austria.

Port Stanley, named after Lord Stanley, afterwards Earl Derby, father of the late Governor-General of Canada, the present Earl Derby. Lord Stanley was visiting Col. Talbot about the time the place was named.

Dorchester (Township) so called as a compliment to Sir Guy Carleton, who was three times appointed Governor General, and held office from 1766 to 1796. For his services he was made a peer of the realm under the title of Lord Dorchester.

www.ingramcontent.com/pod-product-compliance
Lightning Source LLC
Chambersburg PA
CBHW021937160426
43195CB00011B/1130